Edexcel GCSE

History Controlled Assessment

CA8 Crime, policing and punishment in England c.1880–c.1990

Angela Leonard and Martyn Whittock
Series editor: Angela Leonard

A PEARSON COMPANY

Introduction

This unit is about how and why crime, policing and punishment in Britain changed in the years c.1880–c.1990. We shall see that governments passed laws creating new sorts of crime but that most crimes remained remarkably the same, except that criminals developed new high-tech ways of committing fraud and theft.

We shall see that many aspects of policing also stayed the same but that policing methods changed from 1880, when little technology was used, to the high-tech policing of 1990. There have been changes in punishments, too, from harsh punishments, including capital punishment, in 1880. In 1990 there was more emphasis on reform of offenders. A variety of punishments was used as well as imprisonment.

Part A of this book covers:

- changing approaches to punishment

- policing, law and order in the twentieth century

- the changing nature of crime

- developments in investigative policing.

For your controlled assessment in this unit, you will learn how to carry out an enquiry (Part A) and to analyse and evaluate representations of history (Part B). Later sections of this book cover the skills you will need to be successful in unit 4.

Your Part A enquiry will focus in detail on one key question. In Part B you will focus on representations of history: how to analyse, compare and evaluate different views of how effective Victorian policing was.

Contents

Crime, policing and punishment in England c.1880–c.1990

Part A: Carry out a historical enquiry

Part B: Representations of history

A19

Part A Carry out a historical enquiry

A1 Changing approaches to punishment c.1880–c.1990

Learning outcomes

By the end of this topic, you should be able to:

- explain how changing attitudes in government and society can lead to changes in punishment
- show how prisons were reformed in the late nineteenth century
- explain how and why the death penalty was abolished
- describe alternatives to prison and the reasons for introducing these.

'Engines of change'

Changes take place in history for a range of different reasons. The driving forces behind these changes are sometimes called 'engines of change'. They are the things which cause changes to occur. Think of them as being like 'engines' shunting or pushing 'railway trucks'. In this way of thinking about it, the 'trucks' moving forwards are the changes which then happen because of the 'engine of change' pushing.

Within the changing history of punishment, two of these 'engines of change' are (a) government action and (b) changes in society.

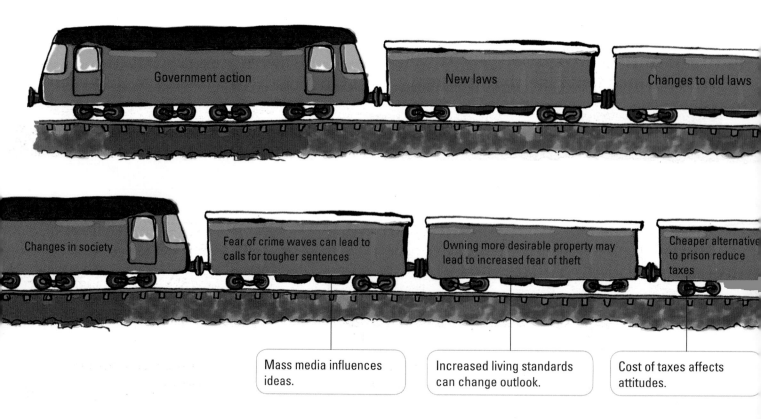

Government action — New laws — Changes to old laws

Changes in society — Fear of crime waves can lead to calls for tougher sentences — Owning more desirable property may lead to increased fear of theft — Cheaper alternative to prison reduce taxes

Mass media influences ideas. — Increased living standards can change outlook. — Cost of taxes affects attitudes.

'Engine of change' 1: government action

Government plays an important part in the changing history of punishment because it is the laws passed by governments which decide that certain actions are crimes and how they are to be punished. As a result, government is one of the very important causes of change. The government may take action which causes change for different reasons, for example:

- new information may make government more aware of a crime, or of the effects of crime
- the cost of a type of punishment may make its use more or less attractive
- types of punishment may become more or less popular with voters.

'Engine of change' 2: changes in society

The opinions of people living in society do not stay the same over time. As these attitudes change, so pressure can build on government to respond and alter the ways in which it acts.

Did you know?

Overall crime figures were lower in 2008 than in the mid-1990s.

When 'engines' collide

It should not be assumed though that these two 'engines of change' always work smoothly together. This is not always the case. For example, public opinion, as measured by opinion polls, is at times favourable to the reintroduction of the death penalty but successive governments have not changed the law to respond to such opinions or pressure.

Activities

1. Interview older friends, members of your family and teachers about corporal punishment in schools: find out what it was, when caning was stopped and why.

2. Choose one of the 'engines of change'. Then, in your own words, explain to a partner what it is, why it is important and how it can lead to changes taking place. Your partner should then do the same for the other 'engine', to you.

3. Explain how the two 'engines of change' do not always work smoothly together. Give an example to show this from information given on these pages.

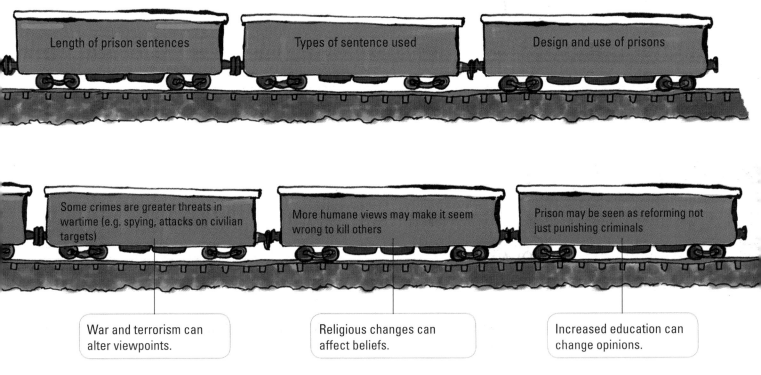

Length of prison sentences | Types of sentence used | Design and use of prisons

Some crimes are greater threats in wartime (e.g. spying, attacks on civilian targets) | More humane views may make it seem wrong to kill others | Prison may be seen as reforming not just punishing criminals

War and terrorism can alter viewpoints. | Religious changes can affect beliefs. | Increased education can change opinions.

The condition of prisons by 1880: the background to change

Prison life was deliberately made hard, including long hours of monotonous work, a poor, boring diet and isolation. Visits from family were allowed only twice a year. The only regular visitor was the prison chaplain, who encouraged the prisoners to be sorry for the crimes they had committed.

Changing prison design: the 'separate system' in the 1880s

Since the 1830s an American idea called the 'separate system' had changed how prisons were organised. They were built so that prisoners could be isolated – kept separate from each other (see Sources A–D).

At first the main aim of the system was to reform prisoners by keeping them alone to think about their crimes. By the 1850s there was evidence that this made some prisoners go mad, though there were also criticisms that prisoners were sometimes able to communicate when isolation was not complete.

By the 1880s the system was still seen as a way of trying to change prisoners by keeping them apart from evil influences and through doing useful work, but there was more emphasis on punishing them for their crimes.

Work and punishment in prisons

After 1865 anyone put in prison for over three months had to do hard labour. This work was intended mainly to punish prisoners for their crimes rather than to provide an income. Prisoners in solitary confinement in some prisons picked oakum. This involved pulling apart tarred rope into its individual fibres. This work damaged the fingers and was very painful. Some solitary prisoners picked rags, separating out different sorts of material and tearing it into strips. Many prisoners were expected to sew prison uniforms, or mail bags, used by the postal service to hold letters. Those in prisons near quarries broke stones.

Many prisoners walked on the treadmill. This was a large iron frame of steps around a revolving cylinder.

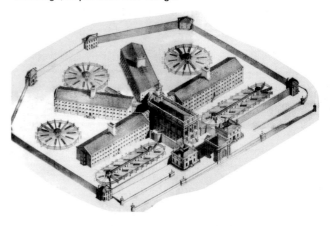

Source A: Prisons such as Pentonville were multi-storied buildings, separated into wings.

Source B: Prison cells were entered from galleries surrounding large open landings like those shown in this drawing of the inside of Pentonville Prison. This allowed a small number of warders to control many cells.

Source C: Even during exercise, prisoners were kept some distance apart from each other and some had to wear masks, as shown in this drawing of prisoners exercising at Pentonville.

Prisoners walked on the treadmill for up to six hours a day. They were separated from other prisoners by a partition. At this stage in most prisons the treadmill had no useful purpose and was just lonely, exhausting and monotonous hard work. Some prisons in England, though, adopted the treadmill as a form of hard labour that could also provide power to grind grain and so make the prisoners' efforts useful.

This hard labour was a normal part of the harsh conditions of prison life but prisoners were also punished for misbehaviour by **flogging**.

> **Flogging**: a harsh form of corporal punishment that was used for serious rule breaking.

Criticism of the harsh prison conditions of the 1880s

The 'separate system' and other forms of harsh treatment were causing concerns by the late 1880s. There was evidence that it made people insane and also that many prisoners committed suicide. A number of critics felt that prison conditions were, on the one hand, too brutal and, on the other, did not succeed in stopping criminal behaviour.

Activities

4. Imagine you are a prisoner in Pentonville prison in 1880. Members of your family are visiting you on one of the few visits allowed a year. Explain to them why so many prisoners hate the 'separate system' and why it has driven so many to suicide.

5. Now imagine that you are the governor of this prison. Explain how you would justify the way you run the prison. In your explanation include:
   - what the 'separate system' is designed to achieve and why you think it is right
   - the way in which the prison is designed to assist in your managing of the prisoners
   - your explanation of why and how work and punishment should be used to deter crime and to punish inmates.

Source D: In the 'separate system', prisoners were often kept alone in their cells to stop them mixing and learning criminal skills from each other. Many of them worked in their cells, for example weaving on a loom.

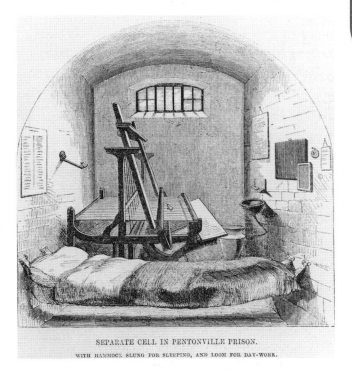

SEPARATE CELL IN PENTONVILLE PRISON.
WITH HAMMOCK SLUNG FOR SLEEPING, AND LOOM FOR DAY-WORK.

The Gladstone Committee,1895

Concern at the effects of harsh treatment on prisoners led to a government investigation called the Gladstone Committee, in 1895. The committee advised the government that:

- prisoners between 16 and 21 years of age should not be subjected to the harsh treatment given to older prisoners
- younger prisoners should be given education and industrial training while in prison
- long periods of silent isolation were not reforming prisoners but were actually having a terrible effect on their mental health.

Follow up your enquiry

What is your local prison like? When was it built? If it has changed since it was first built, how is it different today, compared to when it was first built?

As a result of the advice given to the government by the Gladstone Committee some important changes were made to prison life:

- The time prisoners could be kept in isolation was reduced.
- Prisoners were allowed more time to communicate with each other.
- By 1898 *unproductive* hard labour was abolished – there should be a product from the work.
- In 1902 the first prison designed for young offenders was set up at Borstal in Kent. After 1908 these youth prisons (or 'Borstals') were set up across the country.
- By 1922 it had been generally accepted that solitary confinement should only be used to discipline prisoners who had seriously broken the prison rules. However, corporal punishment for breaking prison rules was not abolished until 1967.

Changing prison design: 1960–1986

By 1950, the prison population was increasing and more new prisons were needed. These new prisons, built in the 1960s, followed a very different design from the prisons of the late nineteenth century – though all the old Victorian prisons continued to be used.

The first of these new prisons was built at Blundeston Prison (Suffolk) in 1963 and its plan was soon adopted at five other sites. Prisons like this continued to be built until the 1980s.

Problems with the '1960s prisons'

The new prisons built in the 1960s were not perfect. The short corridors had poor electric lighting and small windows. They made prisoners feel shut in and were hard to supervise. They were often poorly built.

Source E: Blundeston Prison (Suffolk), built in 1963, was typical of a new style of prison building.

Groups of prisoners were offered training, education and treatment programmes which they attended together.

The aim of organising prisons like this was to encourage prisoners to get on better with each other and also with the prison authorities.

The 1960s prisons were split up into small wings or units.

Each wing on each floor housed up to 16 prisoners.

Changing prison design: the 1980s

In the 1980s prison design changed again. Attempts were made to use the best features of previous designs. This new type of prison had the open landings of the Victorian prisons but also allowed prisoners to be grouped together as had been done in the 1960s.

Source F: Standford Hill Prison (Kent). A new wing built here in 1986 was typical of new thinking about prison design.

These prisons are more open-plan than those in the 1960s and this makes it is easier for prison staff to supervise prisoners.

The shape and look of the 1980s prison is more like the older Victorian prisons – but the prisoners are not kept on their own as they were in the 'separate system'.

In the 1980s-style prisons, groups of prisoners living in each wing had greater freedom to move about their area.

Victorian prisons still in use

Despite these changes, the new prisons of the 1960s and the 1980s did not simply replace the Victorian ones and many of these older prisons are still also in use. As a result, the majority of prisoners in the twenty-first century are most likely to experience a Victorian prison at some point in their sentence.

ResultsPlus

Top Tip

Students who do well can explain that, though new prisons in the 1980s have some features similar to late-nineteenth-century ones, this does not mean a return to old ways of doing things in prisons.

Activities

6. Explain how the design of prisons slowly changed between 1895 and the 1960s. You could think about, for example, layout, use of punishment, interaction of prisoners.

7. Describe the ways in which prisons built in the 1980s developed from the experiences of *both* the late nineteenth century *and* the experiences of the 1960s, in how to build prisons and treat prisoners.

The abolition of the death penalty

At the same time as people were becoming concerned at harsh treatment used in prisons, more people also began to question whether it was right to use **capital punishment**. This was the usual punishment for murder. Between 1948 and 1965 the campaign against the use of the death penalty grew.

> **Capital punishment:** the death penalty – executing (killing) a person as a punishment for a crime.

The background to change

Demands for change after 1948 did not come from nowhere – doubts had been growing about the use of the death penalty for some time. For example, in 1908 the execution of under-16s was stopped due to a growing feeling that younger people might not be fully aware of their actions. In 1933 the age was raised to 18 (at the point when the crime was committed).

> **Humane:** using kindness, mercy and compassion.

These changes in the use of the death penalty were important because they happened for **humane** reasons. Once such reasons had been successfully used to question some uses of the death penalty, it was easier to use humane reasons to challenge the use of the death penalty entirely. This is what happened after 1948. But it is important to remember that changes had already started to occur even before this date.

Arguments in the campaign to end the death penalty

There are a number of both moral and practical arguments for and against the use of the death penalty.

The case for capital punishment:

- If you murder someone, you deserve to die.
- It deters others from murder.
- It gives justice to victims and their families.
- It stops a murderer from killing again.
- It is expensive to keep a murderer in prison.

The case against capital punishment:

- It is always wrong to take a human life – even the life of a murderer.
- What if the wrong person is convicted by mistake?
- Capital punishment does not deter murderers.
- What if a person has acted after having been greatly provoked?
- Some people are mentally ill or do not understand the seriousness of their actions.

A series of controversial executions

The arguments about the use of the death penalty were made more urgent after 1948 by a series of controversial executions. These cases made many people uneasy with the use of this punishment and assisted in finally convincing parliament that it was right to abolish it.

Timothy Evans, 1950: Evans was hanged for killing his baby daughter. (He was not actually charged with killing his wife, though she was murdered too.) Later evidence revealed that Mrs Evans (and at least five other women) had really been murdered by a man named Christie, who lived in the same flats as the Evans family. Evans was **posthumously pardoned** in 1966.

Derek Bentley, 1953: Derek Bentley (aged 19) and Christopher Craig (aged 16) broke into a London warehouse in 1952. Craig shot and killed a policeman. Derek Bentley had serious learning difficulties and a mental age of 11. Both men were found guilty of murder but only Bentley was executed because Craig was under 18 years old. Bentley was posthumously pardoned in 1998.

Ruth Ellis, 1955: On 13 July 1955 she became the last woman to hang. This became a very controversial case because she had suffered violent abuse from the boyfriend she shot. However, the killing was planned, Ellis was sane and she emptied the gun of its bullets into the man. As a result, the jury had no choice but to find her guilty. But the case made people very unhappy that no other sentence seemed available.

The impact of these cases

The public concerns at these controversial cases put pressure on parliament to reconsider the use of the death penalty. But the process of abolition was slow as the arguments were strongly argued on both sides. As a result of this, the changes in the law which would finally stop the use of the death penalty moved forwards in a series of stages.

The stages on the road to abolition

- 1957: a change in the law limited the death sentence to five types of murder.
- 1965: a change in the law suspended the use of capital punishment, but allowed another vote on it in five years.
- 1969: parliament finally abolished capital punishment for murder in Great Britain, though it remained on the statute book for certain other crimes, for example espionage and treason, for many more years.

Further changes after 1969

In 1971, arson in Royal Dockyards stopped being a capital offence. No one would have been executed for it but, until this date, it had still technically been available as a sentence. In 1973 capital punishment was also ended in Northern Ireland.

Posthumous pardon: being found not guilty after having been executed.

Activities

8. Choose *one* of the following individuals and explain how that person's execution was important in changing attitudes towards capital punishment:
   - Timothy Evans
   - Derek Bentley
   - Ruth Ellis.
9. Construct a timeline of the main events between 1948 and 1969 which led to the abolition of the death penalty. Then use this timeline to explain why public concern about the use of the death penalty grew among some members of society and in parliament.

ResultsPlus
Watch out!

Do not describe the abolition of capital punishment as if it was just due to the final change in the law in 1969. There can be a danger of focusing on this final event, rather than explaining how the law gradually changed to finally reach this point.

Reform and rehabilitation

During the second half of the twentieth century, prison reformers have continued to argue that what was needed was more education, getting offenders off drugs and preparing them for returning to society. Many do not see prison as the best way to treat non-violent offenders. These ideas have had an effect on public opinion over time.

These arguments and changes in public opinion have caused governments to change laws and advice to judges on sentencing. They have also led to attempts to improve education and drug treatment in prisons. As prison is expensive and – even when accompanied by education programmes – often does not reform criminals, alternatives to prison have become more common.

Alternatives to prison

Do we need to send all criminals to prison – or just the ones who have committed serious offences? Is prison necessary for all offenders? Some of the reasons why prison is not always seen as the best way to treat offenders are shown below.

Reasons for finding alternatives to prison

Activities

10. Look at the 'Reasons for finding alternatives to prison'. Which would you say are the top three reasons from this list? Explain why you think these are the most important reasons for finding alternatives to prison. Compare your ideas with a partner.

11. Read the information on pages 12–14. For each of the following, explain how it can be argued that it makes punishment of criminals more constructive and effective: parole, community sentences, probation centres.

Better for criminals to repair the damage they've done.

Prison often does not change criminal behaviour.

Promise of an early release may improve behaviour in prisons.

Better for criminals to see the effects of their crime on victims.

Tackling causes of crime – like few qualifications and poor social skills – is better done in the community.

Prison is expensive.

12

Parole

One alternative is parole. It was first introduced by the Criminal Justice Act of 1967 as one of a number of ways to **rehabilitate** prisoners. Parole means releasing prisoners early from prison if it is felt that they do not pose a threat to the public.

However, concerns grew that too many prisoners were being released and so in 1983 a stricter approach was adopted for prisoners serving sentences of over five years for violent or drugs trafficking offences. These prisoners were only to be granted parole when it could be shown that release from prison a few months before the end of a sentence was likely to reduce the long-term risk to the public.

At the same time, the term of a life sentence was made longer, along with stricter rules governing when they might be released early.

Later, under the Criminal Justice Act of 1991, a more centralised Parole Board was given the power to order the early release of certain classes of prisoner. These were those prisoners serving sentences of between four and seven years.

Community sentences

As a result of new thinking about alternatives to imprisonment, which had its origins in 1907 with the formation of the Probation Service, modern courts do not always use prison as a form of punishment. In 2003, 'community orders' were introduced. These could require offenders to attend drug or alcohol treatment programmes, work on community projects, work for charities or repair damage to property and remove graffiti. Programmes like these aim to make offenders understand the effects of their crimes.

Rehabilitate: to restore to useful life.

Source H: *Punishment in the community: managing offenders, making choices,* Anne Worrall and Clare Hoy, 2005.

> There were limits on the levels of participation that could be required of someone whose attendance was compulsory. Offenders could be compelled to attend and sit in a room with an instructor or trainer. But they could not be compelled to talk about themselves and certainly not to discuss any problems or behaviour which they might consider intimate or confidential.

Source I: Based on information in the Crime and justice section of the government website (www.direct.gov.uk).

> Community sentences have three important impacts on criminals. The criminals will either:
>
> 1. do unpaid work
> 2. get job training
> 3. receive psychological help (or all three).

Source G: Young people on a community sentence, cleaning graffiti.

Follow up your enquiry

Find examples, from local papers, of crimes and sentencing (a) which did involve prison and (b) which didn't. In your opinion why was prison used in some examples and not in others?

Probation centres

These centres were set up from the early 1980s as alternatives to prison which still allowed probation officers opportunities to both monitor and control the behaviour of offenders. By building larger centres it became possible to hold group meetings as part of programmes designed to change criminal behaviour and confront the issues which lead to crime. It also provided ways to improve the education of those made to attend and to explore ways of using leisure time in a positive and constructive way.

However, these centres are controversial. Actually getting a person to confront the things in their life that are leading to crime can be very difficult. Also, it has been claimed that, where probation centres have been sited in residential areas in a number of places in England, there has been an increase in crime and anti-social behaviour nearby. This has made many people reluctant to have such a centre in their neighbourhood.

Activities

12. Read Source H. In your own words write one sentence which sums up these researchers' concerns about whether probation centres were effective.

13. What other concerns are there about the use of this particular alternative to prison? Do these concerns seem reasonable to you? Look at the information on pages 13–14 before you write your answer.

14. Look at the reasons for community sentencing, outlined in Source I. Decide (a) which are based on the idea of punishment as a deterrent and (b) which are based on the idea of punishment as a way to reform and rehabilitate criminals.

Your conclusion so far

From this topic we have seen that:

- Changing attitudes in society and government have altered the way in which prison is used as a form of punishment.
- These changes had a similar effect on the use of the death penalty, leading to its abolition.
- The most modern example of these social changes has been the way in which alternatives – which are thought to be more constructive than imprisonment – have been used as punishments for crime.

From what you have learned in this topic so far, how much has changed in approaches to punishment since 1880?

To answer this question:

- explain how prisoners were treated in prison in 1880
- show how this changed
- link this change in attitudes towards punishment to the abolition of the death penalty
- explain how, in the late twentieth century, alternatives to prison were used
- decide how much has changed between 1880 and 1990.

A2 Policing, law and order in the twentieth century

Learning outcomes

By the end of this topic, you should be able to:

- understand some of the key challenges facing policing in the twentieth century
- explain the ways in which the police have had to respond to the use of firearms by criminals
- explain how public-order challenges have caused the police to adapt and use new tactics.

What kind of police force?

The police service, as it was set up in the nineteenth century, was designed to provide police forces indifferent parts of the country as an alternative to the army for keeping public order and deterring crime. Increasingly it also gained a role of detecting crime through its **CID** units.

The kind of police force that this produced was often unarmed (though the Metropolitan Police were usually armed with revolvers in the 1880s and 1890s) and required the cooperation of the public to carry out its duties. As the twentieth century progressed, a number of issues arose which challenged this kind of police force. As a result, the police service has faced the difficult balancing act of maintaining public confidence while working to meet challenges that were not really thought of when it was set up in 1829. A number of these challenges are given here, and over the rest of this topic we will be exploring how the police force has changed and adapted in response to these challenges.

> **CID:** Criminal Investigations Department of the police.

Challenges to policing in the twentieth century

Source A: Police in riot gear, 1984.

Armed criminals

Ethnic tension in a multi-cultural society

Armed political groups

Whether the police should be allowed to protest to get improvements in their pay and conditions

How to police violent industrial disputes or large-scale public protest

Activity

1. Look at the challenges facing the police in the twentieth century. Which of these new challenges do you think the police would find it hardest to deal with?

How should the police respond to the use of guns?

The Siege of Sidney Street, 1911

During the nineteenth century the police had had to recognise that there would be times when the criminals they faced would be armed with guns. This was a real challenge to a force which was designed to be unarmed. In the 1880s, after police had confronted a number of armed burglars, thousands of Metropolitan Police carried pistols on the beat but, as the fear receded, these were gradually withdrawn. During the twentieth century this threat from armed opposition to the police – from both political extremists and criminals – increased.

In 1911 there was a serious challenge to the unarmed police. The response of the authorities raised questions about just how prepared the police were to react to such a challenge. This event is known as 'The Siege of Sidney Street'. The Siege of Sidney Street was carried out by immigrants from Latvia. They were revolutionaries as well as being criminals.

Countdown to confrontation:

- 16 December, 1910, the 'Gardstein gang' attempt to rob a jeweller's shop, in the Houndsditch area of London.
- They kill three unarmed policemen and injure two others when interrupted.
- 2 January, 1911, the Metropolitan Police receive information that two of the Gardstein gang are hiding at 100, Sidney Street, Stepney, London, in the flat of Mrs Betsy Gershon.

Did you know?

The two sides in the confrontation at Sidney Street were not equally armed. The police were armed with revolvers, shotguns and rifles fitted with barrels normally used on a miniature firing range. On the other hand the Latvian gunmen were armed with Mauser pistols. These were capable of fast and deadly fire (though they were not nearly as powerful as the rifles used by the Scots Guards).

The response of the police:

- 3 January, 1911, 200 police cordon off the area and evacuate other residents.
- At dawn, Inspector F. P. Wensley, of H Division (Whitechapel) police, goes with several officers to knock on the door. Pistol shots, from inside, hit Detective Sergeant Leeson. He is rescued by the unarmed Inspector Wensley.
- Police rescue Mrs Gershon.
- The **Home Secretary**, Winston Churchill, goes to Sidney Street to take command.
- 21 **marksmen** of the Scots Guards arrive from the Tower of London.
- The Scots Guards fire into the upper rooms of 100, Sidney Street. The gunmen are forced downstairs by the gunfire.
- Then more Scots Guards – placed across the street – fire on them.
- Churchill orders in heavy weapons (normally used on the battlefield).
- Before the artillery arrives, the house catches fire. One gunman emerges and is shot.
- The fire brigade arrives but Churchill orders them not to put out the fire.
- The fire destroys the building.
- Two bodies are discovered inside. One man has been shot; the other has died in the fire.

Fact file

The Home Secretary, Winston Churchill, had served in the army in India, the Sudan and in the Boer War. He had also been a war correspondent as well as a politician.

Home Secretary: a senior member of the government, in charge of the Home Office.

Marksman: a person who is skilled in accurate shooting of a firearm.

Source B: Police shelter to avoid being shot by the gunmen in Sidney Street.

Police are poorly armed, compared to well-armed Latvians.

Scots Guards are used to support the police.

Unlike the police, the Scots Guards are well-armed marksmen, skilled in accurate shooting.

The impact of the Siege of Sidney Street

The Siege of Sidney Street raised serious questions of how the police should respond to challenges from armed criminals.

The question of command: Should the Home Secretary have been standing on a street corner within range of the gunmen? Most people agreed that the job would have been better done by a senior police commander on the spot. Such a police officer would need better training to be able to lead in such a situation in the future.

The question of armed police: Few people wanted the police regularly to carry weapons. But most were agreed that they should be armed with better weapons when needed. As a result of the Siege of Sidney Street, the police were equipped with faster-firing Webley semi-automatic hand guns when needed.

It was also argued that the police needed better training in how to deal with such violent situations in future.

Did you know?

A bullet from one of the gunmen went through Churchill's top hat while he was commanding the police. It almost killed him!

Fact file

The Siege of Sidney Street was not the only violent crime involving Latvian immigrants in London. In January, 1909, two Latvian anarchists stole wages being delivered to a factory in Tottenham. As they made their getaway, they shot 21 people, killing a policeman and a 10-year-old boy. They were eventually cornered and committed suicide.

Activity

2. Imagine that you are a senior police officer at the time. You have been asked to write a report about the siege. Your report should:
   - present the evidence of whether the police were prepared for the challenge of the siege
   - explain what was needed in future to better prepare the police to deal with such events.

Controlling guns

Sidney Street – though dramatic – was only one of many challenges which caused the law to change in order to control access to guns.

- The 1937 Firearms Act raised the minimum age for buying a firearm from 14 to 17 years, brought increased controls over ownership of shotguns, made illegal the non-military ownership of machine guns and set rules for gun dealers.

- The 1968 Firearms Act brought together all existing gun laws in a single law.

- In 1988 the Firearms (Amendment) Act became law. This followed the terrible Hungerford massacre of 1987, when a gunman armed with automatic weapons far more powerful than those available to the police murdered 16 people and wounded 15 others. After this, gun control was tightened up even further.

- Following the murder of school children and their teacher by a gunman in Dunblane, Scotland, in 1996, another change in the law in 1997 led to handguns being almost completely banned from private ownership.

Concerns at the growth of 'gun culture'

During the 1970s and 1980s concerns grew over the growth of a 'gun culture' among some young people. This growth was blamed on the way violence was portrayed in the media. A steady rise in violent gun crime continued in the 1990s and remains a matter of great concern 20 years later. Much of it is linked to violence between rival drug gangs in large cities.

The use of guns by the police

The police are reluctant to carry guns, which is nothing new. During the spate of armed burglaries in the 1880s (page 16), the Metropolitan Police allowed police officers to carry a pistol on night duty if they wanted to – but officers were told to keep the gun hidden.

From 1936 these guns could only be issued if the station sergeant thought that the risk justified them being carried. But incidents of armed crime increased and so, in 1966, special training was introduced by the Firearms Department to ensure that some police officers were skilled in using guns.

Source C: A police officer from the specialist firearms unit (SO19).

The response of the police to the threat of guns:

- First 'armed response vehicles' (ARVs) used in London in 1991. These are sent if gun use by criminals is suspected.

- All other police forces now employ ARVs.

- Metropolitan Police Service set up a special firearms unit called SO19, in 1991.

- Special Branch anti-terrorist unit, SO13, available if the threat involves terrorists.

18

But when, in 1987, police were allowed to carry guns openly at Heathrow and other airports, there was a lot of concern at how this changed the character of the police force. During the 1980s there were incidents where the police shot innocent people (such as Stephen Waldorf and John Shorthouse, for example). Such cases helped to tighten up police procedures about how to handle guns but also led to the kind of public worry caused by armed police at Heathrow. Despite this, the increased use of guns by criminals and of terrorist threats (see page 26) has meant that an increasing number of police have guns available, even though the ordinary police constable on duty does not carry one.

Source D: A painting by the graffiti artist Banksy.

Context for Source D

Banksy is a graffiti artist from Bristol. His pictures often raise questions about political and social issues. They are often accompanied by slogans designed to make people think about these issues.

Watch out!

When you are carrying out your own research into the changes in policing caused by gun crime, don't forget that such crimes are still a tiny minority of the total crime figures. Most policing is unaffected by this threat. It is important to keep a sense of proportion.

Follow up your enquiry

The Hungerford Massacre shocked the country and led to changes in the law. What was done after it to tighten up control of ownership of guns in Britain?

Activities

3. Construct a timeline of the dated events. Colour-code it with:
   - one colour for changes in the law designed to control the use of guns
   - a different colour for police responses to the use of guns by criminals.

4. Look at Source C. Explain why it has been necessary for the police to employ officers such as this one from SO19 and the other firearms units of the police. Use the information from this topic to help you organise your answer. Mention specific events and developments from the timeline you have constructed, as well as other factors you think are important.

5. Does carrying guns change the way people feel about the police? Does this matter? You may find it helpful to think about the attitude towards armed police revealed by Banksy, in Source D.

The police strikes of 1918–1919

Most workers at this time had the right to join trade unions but the police did not. Should the police be able to go on strike?

The police play such an important part in keeping law and order that they are not allowed to strike. But in 1918–19, for the first and only time, this was seriously challenged. The way in which the government dealt with this reveals just how worried they were by it.

A law called the Crime Act (1885) had made it illegal for anyone to interfere with the police in carrying out their duty. This slowed down the formation of a police **trade union** because it could be argued that it was illegal to encourage a policeman not to work!

The start of a police trade union

During the First World War, police pay stayed constant but the cost of living rose rapidly. Many policemen had difficulty coping with this situation, and a number of police officers secretly joined a union called the National Union of Police and Prison Officers (NUPPO). Anyone found to be a member was instantly sacked. But, by 1918, NUPPO claimed that it had a membership of about 10,000 police officers in London. This was out of a total of 12,000 police officers serving in London.

The demands of the police union

NUPPO called for better pay, pensions for widows of policemen, more generous pensions, and an allowance to help support school-aged children of police officers. NUPPO also demanded that it should be recognised as the official police trade union.

On 30 August 1918, almost all London police officers went on strike! Troops were called in to control the city. The government was desperate to stop the strike and agreed to most of the police demands – and so the strike was called off.

Most police officers were pleased with what was agreed. Pay increased, police officers no longer had to work for 30 years before getting a pension – the length of time was reduced to 26 years. Police widows were given pensions. In addition, police families were given a grant for each child of school age. But NUPPO would still not be recognised as the official police trade union.

> **Trade union:** an organisation in which workers group together, usually to negotiate pay and conditions with employers.

Source E: Thomas Scott, a leading member of NUPPO in London, was quoted in the *Westminster Gazette*, 30 August 1918. He was commenting on how he felt police complaints were being dealt with by the government.

> We are sick of being messed about and being told that they are being considered, considered, considered.

Source F: Sylvia Pankhurst was quoted in a left wing paper called *Workers' Dreadnought,* 7 September 1918.

> Spirit of Petrograd! The London police on strike! After that, anything may happen. Not the army, but the police force is the power which quells political and industrial uprisings and maintains the established fabric of British society.

Context for Source F

Sylvia Pankhurst was a leading member of the campaign for women's rights and a political commentator on a number of issues. What did she mean when she said 'Spirit of Petrograd'?

Petrograd was the capital of Russia, which had experienced revolution in 1917. Pankhurst hoped that the same ideas and ways of acting might be spreading to Britain. She hoped that events such as the police strike might eventually lead to a revolution here.

The defeat of NUPPO

To defend itself, NUPPO called for another strike in 1919. This time only a small number of London policemen responded, though there was a much bigger response in Liverpool. Without a police force, law and order broke down in some parts of Liverpool and this went on for three or four days. At last the army, helped by police who had refused to strike, brought the situation under control. But about 200 people had been arrested for looting. Every police officer who had gone on the second strike throughout the entire country was sacked.

Building a future without strikes

A new Commissioner of the Metropolitan Police was appointed with instructions to end the power of NUPPO. He was helped by the Police Act of 1919. This new law set up the Police Federation of England and Wales as a group which would represent the police.

But at the same time this law banned police from belonging to a trade union. To make this more acceptable, they received a pay increase that doubled their wages. It was clear the government would not ignore the police any more. As a result of this – despite complaints about pay and conditions – the police have not gone on strike since.

Source G: A comment by the Prime Minister, Lloyd George (to another member of the government), in January 1919. By 'Guardians of Order' he means the police.

> Unless this mutiny of the Guardians of Order is quelled, the whole fabric of law may disappear. The Prime Minister is prepared to support any steps you may take, however grave, to establish the authority of social order.

Source: House of Lords, Lloyd George to Bonar Law, 27 January 1919

Activity

6. How far did the police strikes of 1918–19 really threaten the stability of Britain?

To answer this question:

- Explain why the police were not given the same right to strike as other workers.
- Explain – using the sources and other information – exactly why the police were striking (and think about how much a threat this was).
- Explain – using the sources and other information – how the strike seemed to be threatening revolution.
- Explain how and why the government dealt with the strikes so firmly and the unrest ended so quickly.
- Conclude with deciding how far the strikes really threatened the stability of Britain.

Source H: A policeman commenting to the newspaper *The Morning Post*, 2 August 1919.

> We have had a great deal to complain about in the past, and I believe that the last strike [in 1918] helped us very much, but today we are being treated better than at any time since I joined the force. Our position is quite comfortable now.

Context for Source G

Lloyd George was a member of the Liberal Party and was the British Prime Minister from 1916 until 1922. He had recently led Britain to victory in the First World War but, by January 1919, he was worried that revolutionary ideas might lead to revolution in Britain. As recently as October 1917, he had seen Communist revolutionaries take control of leading cities in Russia. He had no wish to see such things happen in this country.

Policing public order

We have seen that the challenges the police faced were varied. Some, like the question of guns and police industrial action, raise questions about the kind of police force that we want to have.

A similar question arises when we explore the challenges of policing public order and meeting threats of conflict and violence on the streets. When people take to the streets to protest about issues, this provides a particularly difficult challenge to the police. On the one hand, they need to protect the freedom that people value so highly in a democracy. On the other hand, they have to protect law and order and the rights of all citizens. Some of these issues are explored below.

Policing issues raised by public order

In a democratic country people have the right to protest.

In a democratic country people have the right to state their views.

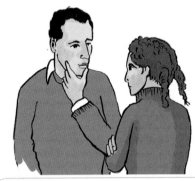

In a democratic country people have the right to disagree with the views of others.

But other people must have the freedom to go about their lives and not be prevented from so doing by protesters.

But one group of people cannot be allowed to intimidate others.

But no one is above the law just because they believe strongly in something.

The challenge of policing public order

In order to explore the challenge of policing public order, we will look at three very different examples, ranging from 1936 to 1985. In each case the cause of the unrest on the streets was very different – and each example posed different challenges to the police. We will look at:

- what happened
- why each challenge occurred
- the response of the police
- questions this raised about the policing of such events.

Example 1: 'The battle of Cable Street', 1936

What happened: on 4 October, 1936, in Cable Street, in the East End of London, the Metropolitan Police, who were supervising a legal march by the British Union of **Fascists**, clashed with a group of anti-fascist protesters.

Why it happened: the racist fascists marched through the East End of London to provoke the local Jewish community. Anti-fascist groups blocked the road.

Police response: the march was legal and the police tried to clear the road to allow it to pass. Fights broke out between police and anti-fascists. The march was abandoned.

Issues about policing

- Should a march be allowed if it threatens others? But should protesters stop the legal rights of another group?

- Following the 'battle' a new law was passed giving the police the power to ban political marches if they felt that public order was threatened. Organisers had to get police permission for their demonstration.

Example 2: Brixton riots, 1981

What happened: on 11 April, 1981, thousands of local residents – mostly from the local Black community – fought police in Brixton, south London. People were hurt (279 police and 45 members of the public), about 100 vehicles were burned and many buildings were damaged.

Why it happened: the area had high unemployment, high crime and poor housing, which particularly affected the Black community. Police attempted to stop street crime by stopping and searching anyone they thought was suspicious, which was very unpopular. Local youths attacked police who, they thought, were arresting a Black youth. This led to fighting on the streets.

Police response: police put more officers into the area, despite the tension. Youths attacked them. More police went in. Petrol bombs were thrown by rioters. A riot lasted until late into the night. Finally 2,500 police restored order.

Issues about policing

- Emphasised the importance of police working with the local community.

- Policing must not be racist.

- Police need proper equipment and training to deal with riots.

> **Fascists:** members of an extreme far-right political group that opposes democracy and believes the state should have total power. It is often associated with racism.

Source I: Cable Street, 1936. Demonstrators retreat as police charge.

Source J: Police battle rioters on the streets of Brixton, south London, 1981. The police were poorly equipped and trained to deal with the violence they encountered. Their plastic shields were not fire-proof and they wore ordinary helmets.

Example 3: The miners' strike, 1984–85

What happened: thousands of coalminers who belonged to the National Union of Miners (NUM) went on strike. Some strikers (called 'pickets') tried to stop other miners going to work. The strike lasted about a year, from March 1984 to March 1985. There was a great deal of violence.

Why violence happened: miners' jobs were threatened by closures of coal mines by the government. The NUM thought those not striking were traitors and the police protecting them were 'enemies', working to defend what the government was doing.

Police response: there was a huge police presence outside the mines. Police charged on horseback to clear miners (for example, during what was known as 'The Battle of Orgreave', Rotherham, June 1984). Police stopped miners acting as **flying pickets** leaving their county to protest outside mines in other counties. Often there was less trouble when local police were used than when police who had been brought in from elsewhere confronted pickets.

Issues about policing

- Have police the right to stop movement of people about the country?
- How much violence should police use?
- Is it better to use local police in local disputes?

Source K: Police on horseback were used against striking miners at 'The Battle of Orgreave', 1984. Police were criticised for using too much force at times.

> ### Did you know?
>
> None of the miners at the Battle of Orgreave was ever convicted of the offences the police charged them with and, in 1991, South Yorkshire police paid out over £400,000 to 39 miners for wrongful arrest.

> **Flying pickets:** strikers travelling to protest in other areas where miners were still working.

Activities

7. In your own words, explain why policing public order is such a challenge.

8. Work in groups of three. Each take a different one of the three examples on pages 23–24. Read your example and look at the sources. Then take it in turns to explain to the others why it occurred and how well you think the police responded.

A new start? 'Newman's Principles of Policing', 1983

The public order problems of the 1980s, and the way in which the police behaved on the streets and related to local communities caused many people to call for a rethink about how policing was carried out.

Sir Kenneth Newman was Commissioner of the Metropolitan Police from 1982 to 1987. He is best known for reorganisation of the Metropolitan Police while he was Commissioner. This reorganisation is known as 'Newman's Principles of Policing'.

What did Newman do?

1. Newman disbanded the controversial Special Patrol Group (SPG). These were London police officers sent round the city to deal with problems including serious public disorder (1961–86). They became associated with violent tactics. During one clash with the SPG, in 1979, a demonstrator named Blair Peach died and the SPG was accused of being involved in his death. The SPG was replaced by the better-trained and better-supervised Territorial Support Group.

2. Newman set up 'area-based policing' to try to get police more in touch with their local communities.

3. He published his Principles of Policing in 1983. This provided new guidelines for how policing should be carried out in London:

- The police should have closer relationships with their communities. There should be a partnership between police and local communities, to work with communities not against them.

- These partnerships could involve **Neighbourhood Watch** schemes, **Crime Prevention Panels**, **Victim Support Schemes**, and the police working with other agencies such as social workers to try to prevent criminal behaviour.

- Officers on duty should have more freedom to decide the best course of action depending on the situation.

Newman's Principles of Policing did not solve the problems facing the police in the complex modern world but they faced up to some, at least, of the serious challenges.

Neighbourhood Watch: an organised group of citizens who work together with the police to prevent crime within their neighbourhood.

Crime Prevention Panels: locally organised groups who work with the police to deal with local crime problems.

Victim Support Schemes: local branches of a national organisation which exists to help people who have been victims of crime.

Activity

9. Sir Kenneth Newman has sometimes been described as being responsible for laying the foundations of modern policing. Explain (a) what he did and (b) why he might be described in this way.

 Your conclusion so far

From this topic we have seen:

- The way in which policing is carried out was challenged by a number of issues in the twentieth century.

- These issues have included: armed crime, police trade union rights and challenges to public order.

- Policing has changed and adapted as a result of these challenges.

From what you have learned in this topic, how much has policing changed as a result of the challenges facing the police in the twentieth century?

To answer this question:

- describe what challenges the police have faced

- explain how well the police were able to meet these challenges

- explain how these challenges caused changes to occur in policing

- decide how much policing has changed since 1900 as a result of these challenges.

A3 The changing nature of crime

Learning outcomes

By the end of this topic, you should be able to:

- explain new crime challenges facing the police in the twentieth century
- identify ways in which the police responded to these new situations
- discuss whether these challenges really are 'new crimes' or old crimes in new forms.

The changing nature of crime

The nature of crime – unfortunately – never stands still. If it did, crime might be easier to prevent, detect and punish. Changes in society provide criminals with new opportunities for crime. Changing kinds of conflict in society give rise to actions which break the law – sometimes dramatically – in new ways.

In all these situations the police have to respond and, where necessary, change their methods and tactics if they are going to be able to meet the challenges of these new criminal developments.

The challenge of terrorism

Terrorism is when groups direct violence at civilians in order to force governments to make changes which will be of benefit to themselves.

This challenge has caused more deaths and disruption than the gun crime and public order challenges discussed in Topic A2 (pages 15–25). This does not minimise the impact of those problems – it simply shows just how terrible an impact terrorism can have on individuals and on society.

Why do some groups use terrorism as a tactic?

It grabs the headlines! People notice the demands of terrorist groups.

It is a way by which small violent groups can strike against a much more powerful enemy – by attacking civilians, instead of soldiers.

It damages the economy of the people that terrorist groups regard as 'the enemy'.

It shows the supporters of the terrorist group that their group can hurt their 'enemies'.

It frightens opponents.

It may cause people to put pressure on their government to meet the terrorists' demands.

The origins of the IRA

Since the nineteenth century various groups within the island of Ireland had used violence to try to force Britain to leave Ireland. The Irish Republican Army traces its roots to a group called the Irish Volunteers, which was formed in 1913. From 1919 the name Irish Republican Army (IRA) was used by those fighting the British in what is known as the 'Irish War of Independence', from 1919–1921.

The IRA after the Irish War of Independence

In 1921 the British government agreed to give independence to Ireland but Northern Ireland remained a part of the United Kingdom. This was because a majority of the community in Northern Ireland wished to stay part of the UK. These were Protestant '**loyalists**', whereas the majority of the population in Ireland as a whole were Catholics.

> **Loyalists:** Irish people who strongly support political union between Great Britain and Northern Ireland.

The IRA splits

The decision to divide the island of Ireland into north and south caused great anger among those who had fought the British to gain an independent Ireland. Some were prepared to accept it as a temporary situation that they could do nothing about. These members of the IRA who (reluctantly) accepted the treaty with Britain then formed the National Army of the new Irish Free State (later to become the Republic of Ireland).

Those who refused to accept it continued to call themselves the IRA. Between 1922 and 1997 they fought: *firstly* the National Army of the Irish Free State in the Irish Civil War (and lost); *then* they fought the British in the hope they would force the end of British rule in Northern Ireland. In 1969 the IRA split again. From 1971 until 1997 they carried out their biggest campaign of attacks against the British government and those loyal to it.

Fact file

Today the Special Branch is a unit of the police whose responsibility is fighting terrorism and other political crime. In 1883 they were originally set up as the 'Special Irish Branch' and were formed to combat a group called the 'Irish Republican Brotherhood' – a group like the later IRA.

Activities

1. Decide on your own definition of terrorism. Vote as a class on the definition you feel best describes it.

2. Explain why some groups use terrorism as a way of campaigning for what they want. Which of the six reasons suggested on page 26 do you think would be most likely to gain success for a terrorist group?

The Republic of Ireland and the United Kingdom. After the Irish War of Independence, 26 counties in the south of Ireland became a separate state, free of British control. The six remaining counties of Northern Ireland stayed as part of the United Kingdom. The island of Ireland was divided.

Scotland

Northern Ireland

Ireland

England

Wales

United Kingdom

Republic of Ireland

The IRA campaigns in the 1930s and the 1940s

In the 1930s the IRA reorganised itself within Northern Ireland and attempted a campaign of bombing on the British mainland and in Northern Ireland. In Northern Ireland it had support among Catholic **Republicans**, who were often badly treated and who wanted a united Ireland.

During the Second World War the IRA tried to get assistance from Nazi Germany, which was fighting against Britain. This did not result in much assistance, since German agents found it difficult to operate in Britain and many IRA leaders had been arrested by the British authorities. Between 1942 and 1944 the IRA carried out a few small-scale attacks on targets in Northern Ireland but they had little effect.

The IRA campaigns of 1971–1998: the 'Troubles'

Background: the 'Border' campaign

Between 1956 and 1962 the IRA carried out a new campaign of attacks against targets in Northern Ireland. This became known as the 'Border' campaign, or the 'Resistance' campaign. It did not achieve very much.

The start of the 'Troubles'

In 1969 the IRA split again. Many of its members felt it had failed to protect Catholics in Northern Ireland from attacks by Protestant Loyalist groups, who had not been brought under control by the police of the Royal Ulster Constabulary (the RUC). Police officers in the RUC were mostly Protestants and were accused of acting in a one-sided way against the Catholic community. One of the worst riots at this time became known as the 'Battle of the Bogside'. This is an area of the city of Londonderry (called Derry by the Catholic community).

Those who broke away called themselves the Provisional IRA (PIRA). Those left in the old organisation called themselves the Official IRA (OIRA). Eventually the OIRA gave up its armed struggle against the British and ceased to be a threat. But for the Provisional IRA the fight was just beginning. From 1970 the violence increased. This conflict is known as the 'Troubles'.

> **Republicans:** Irish people who believe strongly that Ireland should be reunited as a single country, independent of Great Britain.

Follow up your enquiry

Carry out research into a part of the RUC called the 'B-Specials' and look for criticisms of how they did their policing.

Source A: A painting on a house in the area known to the local Catholic community as 'Free Derry'. It shows the kind of violence seen on the streets during the 'Battle of the Bogside' and other clashes with the RUC, and eventually with the British Army, in Northern Ireland.

Policing the 'Troubles' in Northern Ireland

In Northern Ireland the violence posed huge problems for the police. Protestant loyalist terrorist groups attacked civilian members of the Catholic community. The IRA, on the other hand, targeted all members of the (mainly Protestant) security services, and people they claimed were helping them. They also attacked buildings in a general campaign of destruction.

Protestants and Catholics tended to live in different areas. RUC officers could live near Protestant loyalist areas relatively safely. But the few Catholic RUC officers were easy targets for the IRA if they lived in Catholic areas. This ended community policing in Catholic areas and it became hard for the RUC to gather information.

The RUC were often ambushed where it was hard to fight back. Off-duty RUC officers were murdered at home.

The RUC had to patrol in armoured Land Rovers protected by the Army – often 12 soldiers to one RUC officer.

Ways in which the 'Troubles' changed policing in Northern Ireland

Police stations were turned into forts. This separated the police even more from the Catholics. The IRA did all they could to use this separation to get more support from Catholic communities.

Internment (imprisonment without trial) of people accused of membership of terrorist groups (usually Republicans) was used from 1971 to 1975. This tended to increase sympathy and support for the IRA in Northern Ireland because many republicans and others felt it was wrong to imprison people without a trial.

RUC units were accused of killing IRA members rather than trying to arrest them. This was called 'shoot-to-kill'. Several police chiefs came from Britain to investigate this.

The Special Branch in Northern Ireland had to learn new ways of spying on people and using bugging equipment to listen-in.

There was a big emphasis on recruiting informers to try to get information on IRA plans.

Activities

3. Imagine you are an RUC officer in the 1970s. You are telling a police officer from Britain how different it is to be a police officer in Northern Ireland. Explain how IRA terrorism has changed your job as a police officer. Mention:

   - problems of getting information
   - problems you face at home
   - tactics you have to use to stay safe and the problems these cause you
   - new skills you have had to learn
   - new ways of treating people suspected of being terrorists.

4. Now, imagine you are a member of the IRA. Look at the changes the RUC officer says you have caused to policing. Which changes do you think have *helped* and which have *harmed* your cause most?

IRA attacks on the mainland of Britain

The IRA also carried out bombing attacks on mainland Britain (the island that contains England, Scotland and Wales). They attacked army bases, the government and civilians. They hoped that this would make the British government want to get out of Northern Ireland.

Famous – and bloody – attacks included the 'Birmingham pub bombings' (1974) and the 'Brighton bombing' (1984) – an attempt to kill all members of the Conservative government.

In order to combat this challenge, huge efforts had to be put into watching suspects, examination of clues for evidence after bombings and use of armed police to guard targets and hunt down members of the IRA.

On mainland Britain the police were supported in their work by the vast majority of the population and this greatly assisted them in this dangerous work. This was very different from the much more complicated situation that the police faced in Northern Ireland.

IRA attacks continued until the political agreement called the Good Friday Agreement (1998). This set out how Northern Ireland would govern itself through the elected Northern Ireland Assembly, and also gave an amnesty for convicted terrorists who accepted it. Since then, there have still been attacks by groups, such as the 'Continuity IRA' (a breakaway IRA group), but violence has greatly reduced.

Activities

5. (a) Make a timeline of the main events in IRA activities, from 1919 to 1998 (from pages 27–30).

    (b) Identify any which you would describe as 'turning points' (points of major changes in history).

    (c) Explain why you chose these particular dates.

6. Carrying out historical research sometimes involves reading complex sources of evidence that were not written for school students. Read Source C carefully. Using a maximum of 40 words rewrite this source in your own words to show you understand what it says.

7. What can you learn from Sources B and C about the problems of policing Northern Ireland during the 'Troubles'? Why would this have made carrying out the job of a police officer so difficult?

8. What was the impact of the IRA on policing mainland Britain? Explain with examples from this page.

Source B: *The Edge of the Union: The Ulster Loyalist Political Vision*, Steve Bruce, 1994. Catholic RUC officers were often regarded as 'traitors' in republican areas because they were working for the British government. The IRA felt it would be supported in these areas if it targeted them.

> Catholic RUC men are more popular victims [targets] for the IRA than are Protestants in the police.

Source C: 'The Royal Ulster Constabulary and the terrorist threat', Neil Southern, in James Dingley (ed), *Combating Terrorism in Northern Ireland*, 2009.

> In militant republican areas where popular support for the IRA was strong, the RUC had little … community cooperation. This improved the operational capacity of the IRA. Neither was it easy for the RUC to make inroads into such communities despite having a Communities Relations Branch. As a matter of priority, the IRA could not afford to allow… neighbourhood-style policing… [to build]…inter-personal relationships between RUC officers and members of the local community.

Did you know?

Pressure to catch those responsible for IRA bombings sometimes led to people being wrongfully imprisoned. Examples include the so-called 'Birmingham Six', released from prison in 1991, and the 'Guildford Four', released in 1989.

Source D: Damage caused by a terrorist bomb blast in Ealing, London.

Effects of the IRA attacks

The IRA bombing campaigns on mainland Britain had big effects on policing and society on the mainland (though not as great as in Northern Ireland). Some of these effects are shown below.

New skills had to be developed and used in examining fragments of evidence to trace the people who planted bombs	Surveillance systems – such as the ring of cameras around the City of London, which are now permanent	Undercover operations to watch people suspected of being linked to IRA terrorists	Army had to be used to defuse bombs
Huge damage to property	Police had to carry guns more than before	Civilian deaths	Police and army had to work closely together	Disrupted life in major cities

The influence of technology on crime

As technology changes it can create new kinds of crime. This is because new technology gives people opportunities to do things in a way that they could not before. As problems occur, the law often has to be changed in order to deal with new behaviour that threatens society in some way. Some of the problems caused by increased use of cars are shown on this page.

Laws have changed to try to stop these problems happening. The police have had to change their way of operating in order to police these new crimes and catch offenders.

Did you know?

In Germany, Lebanon, Peru and Venezuela, some of the motorways do not have a speed limit. The Isle of Man does not have a general speed limit on roads, and Australia's Northern Territory has no speed limit outside major towns.

Activities

9. In a small group, try to think of actions committed by criminals today which could not have been done 100 years ago. Then explain to the rest of the class why these would not have happened *in the past* but why these occur *now*.

10. After the whole class has reported back, decide which of these crimes are due to (a) changing social attitudes and which to (b) new technology.

Increased speed of cars has led to more accidents. These affect other road users and pedestrians.

Car insurance has become necessary to pay for injury and damage if an accident occurs. It is illegal not to have it.

Problems caused by the increased use of motorcars in the twentieth century

Alcohol and driving do not mix. It has become clear that even small amounts of alcohol make a person more likely to cause an accident.

Cars are desirable objects. Sometimes they are stolen. (Sometimes called 'twocking': 'taking without owner's consent'.)

Traffic congestion causes problems in busy towns, especially if cars are parked badly or for long periods of time.

Changes in the law and policing caused by the use of motorcars

1925: it became an offence to be drunk in charge of a mechanically driven vehicle

1930: compulsory motor insurance was brought in

1934: police cars got radios to help them intercept getaway cars

1991: a new law of 'Causing death by driving while under the influence of alcohol or drugs' was brought in

1934: a speed limit of 30 miles per hour was set for roads in built-up areas

1977: speed limit – on dual carriageways 70 miles per hour; on single carriageways 60 miles per hour outside built-up areas

1935: first compulsory driving test was introduced for cars

1956: yellow lines first introduced to restrict parking

1967: the first legal drink-driving limit was set

1967: breathalysers were introduced to test alcohol level in a motorist's breath

1965: a 70 miles per hour limit was set for all roads outside built-up areas

From 1960s: faster police cars were introduced to pursue speeding and stolen cars

1960: first traffic wardens gave fines for illegal parking

Activity

11. Make a table with two columns and complete it as follows:

- **Column 1** – fill in the problems identified on page 32
- **Column 2** – list changes in the law, or changes in policing that have happened to deal with these problems.

ResultsPlus
Watch out!

When researching 'new' types of crime it is important to identify what factors lie behind such changes. In the case of changes in technology it is important to identify *what problems* these changes led to, *why* these changes were then defined as crimes and *how* policing changed to cope with these changes.

Did you know?

The Automobile Association (AA) was set up in 1905. Its original purpose was to help motorists avoid police speed traps!

Computers and crime

In 1975, the first personal computers were sold as kits to be put together by customers! In 1976, Queen Elizabeth II sent the first royal email message. Since then the use of computers has grown amazingly – and with this new technology have come new opportunities for crime.

New forms of criminal activity

Computer technology can be used to carry out many new forms of criminal activity:

- storage of illegal images on a hard disk instead of in print
- illegal downloads of music and other forms of piracy
- 'phishing' – using spoof emails to direct a computer user to a fraudulent website in order to illegally transfer money, passwords or credit card details
- 'hacking' (gaining unauthorised access to a computer)
- using a 'virus' (malicious software) to damage or delete stored data
- stealing a credit card number.

Source E: A 1980s personal computer. It was the start of a new way for many people to store and send information. With that new technology, came new opportunities for crime.

Watch out!

Do not assume that just because a crime is being carried out in a new way that it really is a 'new' type of crime. Many crimes are simply new ways of doing 'old' crimes. Stealing a car is really no different from stealing a horse. Identity theft using computers is only a new way of pretending to be someone else. The crime is similar. It is just the method of doing it that has changed.

Activity

12. Set up a class debate. The debate topic is: '*The twentieth century saw the growth of new crimes as a result of new technology*'.

- One group researches the case that *agrees with this viewpoint*. Look at the information on pages 32–35. Add any other information and examples that you think are relevant. Remember that, as well as giving examples of 'new' crimes, you will also have to explain why they really are new.

- The other group researches the *argument against this view*. Think about how these crimes are not as 'new' as they appear. To do this you will need to think about what older crimes were very like these 'new' crimes, and how these 'new' crimes are just new ways of carrying out old criminal activity.

Old crimes or new crimes?

While these crimes may seem 'new', in fact they are really old crimes that use new technology:

- Storing illegal images was done in the past using photographs.

- Harassing someone is not a new activity.

- Impersonating another person (identity theft) is not a new activity.

- Illegally taking money by **fraud** is a very old crime.

- When people paid by cheque, criminals passed forged checks.

Fraud: using deception (trickery) to get a personal advantage or to harm another person.

Did you know?

New laws have had to be created to cope with computer crime. This is because, in older laws, it was assumed that a criminal actually broke into a person's house (or office) to steal. But, with computer crime, the criminal does not actually enter the building. As a result of this, new laws have had to be written which cover stealing through the use of a telephone line to gain access to a computer, without actually entering the victim's house (or office) at any time.

 Your conclusion so far

From this topic we have seen that terrorism has brought new challenges to law and order in the twentieth century.

- In Britain this was seen in the activities of the IRA.

- IRA terrorist activities affected people both in Ireland and on the mainland of Britain.

- The police had to adopt new tactics in order to face this challenge.

Other challenges have come from changes in technology.

- The increase in car ownership and use has required changes in the law and in policing to regulate it.

- Increased computer use has created new opportunities for criminal activities.

- However, many of these new crimes are old crimes done in a new way.

From the evidence you have explored in this topic, explain (with examples) how far the nature of crime has changed in the twentieth century.

1. Describe some of the new challenges to law and order that have occurred in the twentieth century.

2. Explain what kinds of problem these changes have caused.

3. Explain how the law and policing have changed in order to respond to these new challenges.

4. Finally, conclude how far it is correct to describe these challenges as 'new' crimes.

A4 Developments in investigative policing, c.1880–c.1990

Learning outcomes

By the end of this topic, you should be able to:

- explain why the CID was set up in 1878 and how they assisted in detecting crime

- describe the increasing use of forensic science, fingerprinting and other forms of technology by the police from the end of the nineteenth century – and also explain the differences these changes made to the work of the police

- explore the use of technology in the conviction of Dr Crippen in 1910, and investigate the strength of the evidence used to convict him.

Police shortcomings in 1880

When the Metropolitan Police Force was set up in 1829, its main job was to keep order on the streets and to deter (prevent) crime. It soon proved its worth. It was unarmed and better at crowd control than the army had been. The presence of police officers patrolling 'on the beat' discouraged criminals. But how effective were the police in the job of actually detecting (investigating and solving) crime?

It is fairly straightforward to make crime harder to commit by patrolling and by stopping fights in pubs on a Saturday night. Chasing and catching criminals who had been seen in the act of committing a crime was likely to lead to their arrest. It was a much harder job to catch criminals who had committed their crime(s) and then left the scene.

Skills needed for crime detection

Crime detection involves a range of skills which ordinary police officers did not necessarily have:

- recognising clues at the scene of a crime

- using these to understand how the crime had been committed and linking these to the person responsible

- interrogating witnesses

- making sense of a range of evidence and presenting this in court

- using available technology to track down criminals.

Follow up your enquiry

To explore the difficulties of detecting crime in the nineteenth century, carry out your own research into police difficulties in tackling: (a) the 'Rode (or 'Road') Hill House murder' of 1860 and (b) the 'Jack the Ripper murders' of 1888.

Activities

1. Why do we have a police force? What does it exist to do? This might seem a rather obvious question, but think about it. In pairs, or small groups, list the reasons for having a police force and what we now expect it to do.

2. Create a 'Changes in detection' flow diagram. Put the following statements into their correct order on this diagram, using the information on pages 36–7: *Police not trained to detect/ Better technology needed to make CID effective/ Police set up to deter crime/CID created/ Detectives not fully coordinated and too few/Detective Department set up.*

   Then use this to describe to a partner *how* and *why* detection changed in the nineteenth century.

The creation of the CID (1878)

The answer to the problem of detecting crime was to create a new type of police officer – detectives. They operated in civilian clothes and investigated crimes by examining the clues, talking with witnesses and suspects. They were less noticeable than uniformed officers.

The Criminal Investigation Department (CID) was formed as part of the Metropolitan Police on 8 April 1878 by Howard Vincent. Though Vincent's boss was the Commissioner of the Metropolitan Police, he could report directly to the Home Secretary – a member of the government – if he wanted to.

Detectives before the CID

There were already a few detectives operating in London since, in 1842, the plain clothes Detective Department had been set up. But there were few of these detectives and they were not under the control of one head.

The new CID

The headquarters of the new CID was in Scotland Yard, in central London. London was divided into districts with 60 Divisional Detective Patrols and 20 Special Patrols. These were commanded by 159 sergeants and above them were 15 Detective Inspectors. The CID were paid a little more money than the members of the uniformed police. Police forces outside London also began to set up special detective forces.

The Special Irish Branch of the CID

In 1883 Vincent set up the Special Irish Branch, to combat Irish terrorists (see page 27). Special Branch would become the first of the specialist units that grew out of the CID.

ResultsPlus
Watch out!

The creation of the CID is a reminder that a change in policing might not immediately lead to improvements. It was not until new forensic science techniques were developed that the CID became really effective.

The effectiveness of the new detectives

The new detectives soon became an important part of the London police force. Using clues from crime scenes and the evidence of witnesses – and particularly informers – they were more effective at detecting crime than uniformed police officers. But there were real limitations to their effectiveness. They could not always recognise, or make the most use of, clues from crime scenes. Only when **forensic science** developed much later would the effectiveness of detecting crime really improve.

> **Forensic science:** using scientific methods and knowledge to discover facts that can be used in detecting crime.

Source A: The CID at work. Top Picture: CID officers disguised as dockers during an investigation into drug smuggling at Limehouse Docks, London, in about 1911. Bottom Picture: the same officers in their best clothing.

The 'Jack the Ripper' murders, of 1888 – a failure in detection

Between August and November 1888, the country was horrified by the 'Jack the Ripper' murders. The appalling killings of at least five women in the East End of London revealed the inability of the police to detect the killer. You will learn more about these killings in Part B of this book, but here we will just briefly examine the impact of the killings on detection.

How to catch a killer in 1888

Without the use of forensic science, or even fingerprinting, the only way to prove someone had committed a murder was one of the following:

- catch them in the act of murder
- find a witness who had seen the killing
- get the suspect to confess.

In most killings these circumstances do not occur. This problem meant that, try as they might, the police could not catch the killer in the act and – despite arresting a number of suspects – they were never able to bring anyone to trial for the murders.

Problems detecting 'Jack the Ripper'

The killings reveal the problems facing police in the 1880s, despite the setting up of the CID in 1878. It was impossible to tell human from animal blood. As a result, in an area where there were many butchers, this meant that traces of blood could not be linked to the killings. Police lacked the technology to decide if a piece of human body posted to a local man was from a Ripper victim. And a piece of possibly important graffiti was removed before it could be photographed.

The use of photography

Despite this, detectives were becoming more skilled in recording crime scenes in 1888. City of London police officers made drawings of the crime scene in the murder of Catherine Eddowes and took many photographs of the victim. They also took photographs of the murdered Mary Kelly, though she was killed in the area policed by the Metropolitan Police. However, she was the only victim who was actually photographed at the scene of the crime, which shows that the importance of recording the crime scene had not been fully understood at the time.

Source B: A rare piece of evidence from *The Illustrated Police News*, showing early detection in action using new technology. This is a drawing recording the photographing of the body of Mary Kelly in November 1888.

Did you know?

While photographs had been taken in the 1830s, it was not until 1884 that the use of photographic film meant that a photographer no longer had to carry heavy photographic plates and chemicals around. It was in 1888 – the year of the 'Ripper murders' – that the first Kodak camera went on sale in the USA. This was a new technology that would soon help in the detection of crime.

The use of forensic science in detecting crime

The early detectives struggled to detect crime because they lacked the technology, methods and skills needed to get information from clues left at crime scenes and to link criminals with their crimes. As methods of forensic science developed, crime detection by the new CID became more effective.

The Belper Committee

The Belper Committee was a five-man Home Office committee, which was chaired by Lord Belper. It met in 1900 to compare the usefulness of two new methods of identifying suspects and solving crimes. These new methods were anthropometry and fingerprinting.

Anthropometry

Anthropometry was a system which involved recording the body measurements of a person to confirm the identity of a suspect. It was invented by Alphonse Bertillon in 1880 and started being used by Scotland Yard in 1894. (See pages 56–57 for more information.)

Fingerprints

A fingerprint is an impression of the ridges on a person's finger. By inking a person's finger, these can be recorded on paper and compared with fingerprints left at a crime scene. Since no two fingerprints are the same, this is a valuable way of identifying a person.

In 1897 a Fingerprint Bureau was opened in British-run Calcutta, India. Working in what was called the Calcutta Anthropometric Bureau (later called the Fingerprint Bureau) were Azizul Haque and Hem Chandra Bose. Haque and Bose were Indian fingerprint experts. These two men set up the way of using fingerprints that was eventually named the 'Henry System', after their supervisor, Sir Edward Richard Henry.

Henry gave a demonstration to the Belper Committee, using 7,000 fingerprints. As a result the fingerprint department of New Scotland Yard was set up in 1901. Since then, fingerprint evidence has identified many suspects and helped to solve many crimes.

Forensic science

As scientific knowledge has increased (assisted by new technologies such as more powerful microscopes) experts called 'forensic scientists' have used a wide range of techniques to study crime scenes and link criminals to crimes. These include analysis of plant pollen, fibres of clothing and DNA evidence from such things as hair or skin. In 1987, for the first time in the UK, a criminal was convicted using DNA evidence.

Specially trained experts called Scenes of Crime Officers, or SOCOs, attend crime scenes to record and examine the evidence. The evidence discovered is then used to investigate these crimes. (Today they are often called Crime Scene Investigators, or CSIs.)

Did you know?

Since 1995, a National Automatic Fingerprint Identification System allows every police force in England and Wales to compare records of fingerprints. In the same year, the DNA National Database Library was also set up, to store DNA evidence.

Activity

3. Imagine you were a member of the Belper Committee in 1900. Write a report in which you explain why you think it is so necessary to look at new methods of investigating evidence in order to improve crime detection. In your report:

   - explain the problems the CID faced in detecting crimes, mentioning problems of the investigation into 'Jack the Ripper'
   - explain how some new methods are proving helpful (e.g. photography)
   - describe the new fingerprinting system and explain why you think it is worth setting up a fingerprint department at Scotland Yard.

Follow up your enquiry

Carry out your own research into the methods used by SOCOs and forensic scientists. Start with the information on this page and on page 40. Write a report on your findings. How different are these methods compared with detection in 1880?

Forensic science in action

Traces of blood on a broken window can be linked to the DNA of the intruder.

Saliva on wine glass contains a DNA connection to a particular person.

Footprints can be linked to a specific pair of shoes.

Pollen, or seeds, in footprints can show where the intruder came from.

Marks on a bullet show it was fired from a particular gun.

Fibres of clothing can be linked to particular clothes worn by an intruder.

Study of wound on head will show what weapon caused it and how the weapon was used.

Hair left in victim's hand can be linked to the attacker via DNA.

Fingerprints on a desk can be linked to a specific person.

The use of new technology

Photography was used to record crime scenes and could also be used to record images of criminals and missing persons to help in identifying them. Since 1900, many other technologies have been used by the police.

Computers

Computers help in sorting information, finding patterns and matching evidence, which saves a huge amount of police time. They help spot information and patterns of evidence that people would miss. The Police National Computer was first introduced in 1975 and holds records on 25 million people. It can alert police to criminals who have committed crimes similar to ones being investigated. Monitoring websites and emails allows the police to hunt for those planning terrorism.

ResultsPlus
Top Tip

When looking at the impact of new scientific discoveries and technologies it is important to explore not only the direct impact of each of them on policing but also the way in which these different factors work together to bring about progress.

The 'Yorkshire Ripper'

The importance of the use of technology can be seen in the case of the 'Yorkshire Ripper', Peter Sutcliffe, who was convicted in 1981 of murdering 13 women and attacking several others between 1975 and 1980.

Before the use of computers by police, evidence was stored on handwritten cards. This information was not easily sifted and links were not made between vital clues. Sutcliffe was actually interviewed nine times, but since all the information was stored in paper form, the fact that Sutcliffe was being investigated by different police officers was not noticed. Sutcliffe's name was even passed to the police by a suspicious friend but this was lost in the huge amount of paperwork. He was finally arrested when police stopped his car because it had false number plates. Only later did the police discover that they had arrested the 'Yorkshire Ripper'.

Mobile police

The use of cars and motorbikes allows police to get to crime scenes faster. One of the biggest changes of the later twentieth century has been taking police off the beat and putting them in cars.

Radio communication

Better communication makes it easier to report issues and call for backup. The first use of miniature police radios was in 1963.

Specialisation within the police force

The increasingly complex job of policing and detection means that many special units of the police have been set up to deal with particular issues or to develop particular skills.

As well as the difference between uniformed officers and the CID, there are:

- officers trained to work with dogs
- gun crime specialists who are trained to shoot
- drugs officers
- officers trained to deal with children.

Activities

4. Write out the following on small pieces of card:
   - Fingerprinting
   - DNA collecting
   - Photography
   - Computers.

   Then, on the back of each card, write brief notes on how each has assisted in improving police investigations since 1880.

   Use these cards to explain to a neighbour the impact of these things. Score each other on how well you think the issue was explained. Score 1–5, with a score of 5 meaning very well explained and clearly linked to the impact on policing.

5. Explain the way the new technologies of motorcars and radios assisted police work in the twentieth century.

6. Look at the cases of 'Jack the Ripper', and the 'Yorkshire Ripper'. For each case, explain how the use of, or absence of, technology affected the success of the investigation.

Did you know?

The Yorkshire Ripper had a police record. If a DNA database had been available in 1975, he might have been identified at the time of the first murder.

Follow up your enquiry

Find out more about the Yorkshire Ripper: go to www.pearsonhotlinks.co.uk, insert the express code 6466P and click on the link to the Yorkshire Ripper.

How sound was the murder conviction of Dr Crippen?

In 1909, Dr Crippen, originally from the USA, was living with his wife, Cora, at 39 Hilldrop Crescent, Camden Town, London. Crippen was not able to practise as a doctor in London, was in financial difficulty and depended on his wife's income as a singer. He was not happy in his marriage and was having an affair with one of his secretaries, Ethel le Neve.

Mrs Crippen vanishes

On 15 December, 1909, Mrs Crippen told her bank she was removing all her money. It seems likely that she had learned about Ethel and was going to leave Crippen. In January 1910, Crippen bought large quantities of Hyoscine hydrobromide, a drug which, in these amounts, causes drowsiness. Cora was last seen alive on 31 January. Over the next three days Crippen pawned his wife's jewellery, Ethel moved into the house and a letter was received by Cora's friends saying she had suddenly gone to the USA. On 24 March the same friends received a telegram from Crippen saying Cora had died while in the USA.

Escape and capture

Friends of Cora were suspicious. They informed the CID at Scotland Yard, who interviewed Crippen and searched the house but found nothing suspicious. Crippen said that Cora had left him and he had lied to avoid the scandal. The police were satisfied but Crippen panicked. He and Ethel left in secret for Belgium and there caught a ship to Canada. Crippen had shaved off his moustache and Ethel was disguised as a boy.

When the police returned to Crippen's house to check a few facts they found he had left. They were now suspicious and under the brick floor of the coal cellar they found human remains. Meanwhile, the captain of the ship on which Crippen and Ethel were sailing grew suspicious. He thought they looked like the newspaper pictures of two fugitives sought by the police. He sent a wireless telegram to the London police. Detectives caught a faster boat and were waiting for Crippen and Ethel in Canada, arresting them on 31 July, 1910.

The remains in the cellar

Only partial remains were found in the cellar. There was no head, arms or legs and no bones, except for what was possibly part of a thigh bone. On one of the pieces of skin there seemed to be a scar, probably the result of an operation. The skin was analysed for the police by a Dr Pepper, assisted by Dr Spilsbury.

Trial and execution

Crippen was tried for his wife's murder. The jury took only 27 minutes to find him guilty and he was sentenced to death by hanging. Ethel le Neve was put on trial four days later. She was found not guilty. Crippen was executed on 23 November, 1910.

Forensic evidence for Crippen's guilt

The following forensic evidence was used in Crippen's trial:

- The skin tissue showed a scar from an operation like the one Cora had.
- Somebody skilled – like a doctor – cut up the body.
- It was an adult body but the sex could not be established.
- The remains had been buried for four to eight months before being found in July 1910.
- There were traces of *Hyoscine hydrobromide* in the body.

Source C: The piece of skin and the evidence quoted by Dr Pepper and Dr Spilsbury at Crippen's trial.

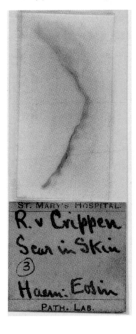

Source D: Report written by Dr Spilsbury, a pathologist, on the finding of the remains below the cellar floor. (Note: Dr Crippen purchased pyjamas, identical to the pyjama jacket mentioned in the source, in January 1909.)

> Human remains found 13 July. Medical organs of chest and abdomen removed in one mass. Four large pieces of skin and muscle, one from lower abdomen with old operation scar 4 inches long. Impossible to identify sex. *Hyoscine* found 2.7 grains. Hair in curler – roots present. Hair 6 inches long. Man's pyjama jacket label reads 'Jones Bros., Holloway', and odd pair of pyjama trousers.

Source: Dr Spilsbury notes on the Dr Crippen case, 1910.

Was the verdict unsound?

Not everyone is convinced that Crippen was guilty. Here are some suggestions as to why he might not have been:

- Crippen may have been giving Cora drugs to calm her but killed her by accident.
- If Crippen had successfully disposed of the rest of Cora's body, why bury parts under the floor where they could be found?
- In October 2007, US forensic scientists claimed that DNA evidence showed that the remains found beneath the cellar floor in Crippen's home were not those of Cora Crippen. The body may have been that of a man. The mark on the skin may not be that from a scar.

Source E: Recent US research on the evidence questions the guilty verdict. From *The Times* newspaper, 17 October, 2007.

> … a team of American scientists who compared mitochondrial DNA from the corpse that was claimed to be Mrs Crippen with that of her living relatives said that the dismembered body was not her… The research team said that a scar on the abdomen of the body, which convinced the jury that the remains were Mrs Crippen's, was incorrectly claimed to be so. But they said that other evidence showed the body could only have made its way to Crippen's house when he and his wife were living there. One of Dr Trestrail's hypotheses is that Crippen was performing illegal abortions and that the body could have resulted from a botched procedure.

Activities

7. Design a 'storyboard' to tell the story of the Dr Crippen murder. This will involve: dividing the story into its main parts, drawing a sketch to sum up each part and, under each sketch, writing a caption to explain each part of the story.

8. Work in small groups. From the evidence you have here: do you think it was right to find Dr Crippen guilty of murder? Explain *why* you think as you do and *why* you are not convinced by the opposite point of view. Then present your findings and conclusion to your class. Vote at the end to decide the verdict of your class.

Your conclusion so far

From this topic we have seen that:

- While the early police were effective at deterring crime, they had difficulty with detecting it.
- The CID was set up to solve this problem.
- The use of forensic science has greatly improved police detection of serious crimes such as murder.
- Other new technologies also assisted the police.
- The case of Dr Crippen shows that forensic scientists do not always agree.
- The 'Yorkshire Ripper' case shows how computer technology is needed to process lots of evidence.

1. From what you have explored in this topic, explain the problems that police detection faced in the 1880s.

2. Then, identify changes which have improved detection and explain how.

3. Finally, decide how different investigative policing was in 1990, compared with 1880.

Enquiry and writing skills support

Learning outcomes

By the end of this section, you should be able to:

- follow up an enquiry
- select and organise your material
- write up your enquiry.

In this section we will see how to complete the stages of following up an enquiry. The diagram on this page shows you the enquiry stages and what you need to do.

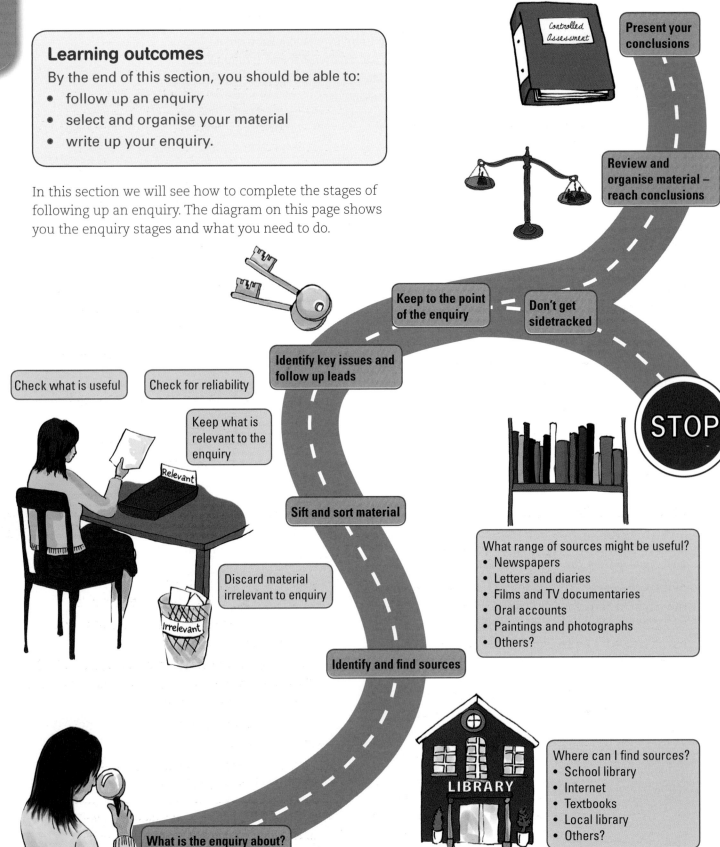

Present your conclusions

Review and organise material – reach conclusions

Keep to the point of the enquiry

Don't get sidetracked

Identify key issues and follow up leads

Check what is useful

Check for reliability

Keep what is relevant to the enquiry

Relevant

Sift and sort material

STOP

Discard material irrelevant to enquiry

Irrelevant

What range of sources might be useful?
- Newspapers
- Letters and diaries
- Films and TV documentaries
- Oral accounts
- Paintings and photographs
- Others?

Identify and find sources

LIBRARY

Where can I find sources?
- School library
- Internet
- Textbooks
- Local library
- Others?

What is the enquiry about?

Controlled Assessment

44

Following up an enquiry 1: The importance of the case of Derek Bentley

Your controlled assessment Part A task will be similar to this one:

> ### Enquiry focus
>
> Your enquiry task will focus on the importance of the case of Derek Bentley in the campaigns to end the death penalty in England.

In this practice example, we are going to follow up the enquiry focus. You will be able to use the skills you develop to follow up your own Part A enquiry.

What is the enquiry about?

Your first step is to identify the precise enquiry. In this instance, it's about the importance of one case (Derek Bentley) as a factor which contributed to the success of the campaign to end the death penalty. This enquiry is trying to find out:

- why the campaign to end the death penalty grew and succeeded in the twentieth century
- why the Bentley case was important in the campaign.

Identify and find sources

The next stage is to gather your information. Start with an easy outline book and read through the relevant material. Write some summary notes, making sure you include the book title, author and the pages where you have found the information. You should only start to look for more in-depth information when you have used two or three textbooks which give you the basic information.

For this enquiry, begin by reading pages 10–11 of this book and completing the activities on this page.

To add to your sources, you might start by doing a quick search on the internet but you should also look at books by historians. When you find a book, check the contents page and the index to make sure it covers the topic you want to research. For this enquiry, you would want to look up 'capital punishment', 'death penalty' and 'Derek Bentley'.

You could also use television documentaries as a source of information but be careful to check them against other sources to be sure they have not been too dramatised or exaggerated.

Sift and sort material

Go through your new sources and make additional notes. It will help if you use a fresh page for each book or other source of information. Remember that the book or the webpage you've found was not written to answer your specific question! For example, this enquiry is about why the Bentley case was important. You have to choose what to take from your source to answer that – see the activity on page 46.

Look for new leads to follow up. For example, Source A (page 46) tells you that the Bentley case was 'significant in the growth of opposition to the use of capital punishment in Britain'. This means it added to the campaign in two ways:

- more people began to worry about the use of the death penalty
- more people began to campaign actively against it.

As you identify new leads, you can follow them up, going through the same process of finding, sifting and sorting and noting information.

Activities

Making notes

1. Make a bullet point list of useful information from your first source of information. For example:
   - doubts had been growing about the use of the death penalty for some time
   - there were controversial executions, e.g. in 1950 Evans was hanged. Later evidence convicted John Christie of murder in the house.
2. Now repeat this process for two other textbooks or simple overviews.
3. Begin to organise your notes. You could sort them into a table like the one below.

Why the Bentley case was important	Why the campaign grew in the twentieth century

Stick to the enquiry path

Don't go off track! On a journey, detours and side roads can be great fun and you can follow them up just because they are interesting. Remember, though, to return to your enquiry path – and not to add in material which isn't relevant. For example, information in Source A about the pardon for Derek Bentley in 1998 wouldn't help you answer an enquiry about the importance of his case in the 1950s.

Source A: *Change in British society, 1955–75,* Nigel Bushnell and Cathy Warren.

The abolition of the death penalty

In the early 1950s the average number of hangings in Britain was about fifteen a year. It was during this period that arguments about the use of the death penalty became much stronger. Two notable cases [the Bentley and Ellis cases] where the death penalty was used were significant in the growth of opposition to the use of capital punishment in Britain.

In 1952 in Croydon, south London, two teenagers were involved in the shooting of a London policeman during a robbery.

The teenager who actually fired the shot was only sixteen and too young to be hanged. The older boy, Derek Bentley, was nineteen. He suffered from learning difficulties. Despite a petition by 200 MPs, he was hanged in January 1953. There was significant public unease that Bentley had been hanged; a nineteen year old with a mental age of eleven and who had not actually fired the gun. This led to a widespread national debate in newspapers, on the television and the radio about the use of the death penalty. Immediately after Bentley's hanging a campaign began to clear his name; this eventually led to an official government pardon in 1998.

Using sources carefully

So far we have applied two tests when using sources: relevance and duplication. Sometimes you will also need to think about reliability. You need to be particularly careful about internet sources because they are sometimes anonymous and it is difficult to check the information they contain. Remember that many internet sites contain opinions without any factual support. Often too they are campaigning, and you need to think about their purpose and possible bias. As you use your sources, apply the RDR tests: **R**elevance, **D**uplication and **R**eliability.

Results Plus

Top Tip

Looking for information can be a slow process. You might read through a lot to get a small piece of new information. But your work is better if you concentrate on what's new and relevant, rather than adding something that duplicates (repeats) information you already have or is not relevant.

Activities

Selecting information

4. Read Source A and decide with a partner how much of it would be useful for this enquiry. Remember:

   * you want to find out why the Bentley case was important
   * usually you only want new points
   * sometimes you may want to make a note that two sources agree about an important point.

5. Copy the passage and colour-code it: green for new information, orange for the importance of the Bentley case and blue for information you already have. Some parts have been done for you.

Activities

Relevance and reliability

6. Study Source B. It is published by a group which campaigns against the use of the death penalty in the USA today.

7. Decide with a partner which of these statements you agree with. Choose as many as you like:

   - It is not biased.
   - It is biased but still has some useful information.
   - It makes statements about whether Bentley was innocent.
   - It makes statements about why Bentley was pardoned 46 years after he died.
   - It makes statements about why Bentley was convicted.
   - It makes statements about why the death penalty ended on Britain.
   - It is mainly relevant to this enquiry.
   - It does not add much to this enquiry.

8. Now that you have completed the relevance and reliability tests on Source B, add any useful information from this to your notes. Remember to avoid duplication – don't repeat information you already have.

Identify key issues and follow up leads

So far this enquiry has provided the following leads (the words in bold could be used as key issues).

- Impact of Bentley case on **public opinion**.
- **Campaign groups** could use Bentley case to increase opposition to the death penalty.
- **Other cases** were also important.
- **Key individuals** campaigned to increase opposition.
- **Parliament** passed the laws to suspend and then end the death penalty.

Source B: The fight for Derek Bentley: a full pardon – 46 years later. *The New Abolitionist Newsletter*, 1998.

The 1953 execution of Derek Bentley, a mentally handicapped 19-year-old who was falsely convicted of murder, was pivotal in bringing about the end of capital punishment in Britain. And now, after 46 years, the British justice system finally admitted its terrible mistake and granted Bentley a full pardon.

The pardon came only because Bentley's family fought continuously since he was hanged. They approached filmmakers, authors and lawyers to urge them to take up the case. As a result, there have been songs, movies and books that made the case widely known. But year after year, the government refused to hold a public inquiry…

It was the judge in the case – Lord Goddard – who made sure that Bentley would be killed. Goddard apparently got perverted pleasure from sending people to death…

At the time of Bentley's execution, Home Secretary David Maxwell Fyfe said: 'There is no possibility of an innocent man being hanged in this country.' But many people in Britain disagreed with him and organized on behalf of Bentley. Two hundred members of parliament signed a motion for Bentley. On the night of the execution, 5,000 people gathered outside the prison chanting, 'Murder!' They fought with police and tore down and burned the death notice that had been pinned to the gates.

A few years later, the government abolished the death penalty in Britain – in part as a response to the outrage around Bentley's case. Now, after nearly a half a century, the British justice system admitted what many people knew all along – that Derek Bentley went to his death an innocent man.

Source C: *Capital Punishment and British Politics*, James B. Christoph, 1962.

The consequences of the Bentley case for the then dormant [not very active] abolitionist movement were considerable. It raised many of the kinds of questions abolitionists wanted raised. Once again there was public unease about the law of murder…

The Bentley and Evans cases aroused public attention because they involved the suspicion that the convicted person did not commit the crime for which he was sentenced. In the third major case [Ruth Ellis] which caused a re-examination of capital punishment, the question was the appropriateness of the punishment. Within a month [after Ruth Ellis' execution] a group of prominent Englishmen formed a new National Campaign for the Abolition of Capital Punishment. They hoped to channel these feelings into a public demand for legislative action…

The Bentley, Evans/Christie, and Ellis cases caught the public imagination. They showed the workings of the law to many people who previously had given scant attention to the question. If the Home Secretaries had chosen other alternatives open to them in each of these cases, the successes of the abolitionists would not have come about.

In this period a large number of politicians, publicists and penal reformers did all they could to keep the names of Bentley, Evans and Ellis well to the fore in any discussion of [reform of] the criminal law. The abolitionists could use these specific cases to help.

Activities

9. Study Source C. It gives two new leads in the areas of the work of campaign groups and the work of individual politicians and reformers.

10. Add information from Source C to your notes. In your real enquiry, it will help if you add page numbers as you build up your notes, in case you want to find the passage again.

11. Identify the key issues whenever you use a new source.

Source file

Source D: From *Let him have Justice*, Iris Bentley, 1996. Iris was Derek's sister.

In 1954 a play about Derek's case came to London. *Murder Story* was written by Ludovic Kennedy and Derek's case was, he says, the reason he first became involved in miscarriages of justice… It doesn't have a character called Derek Bentley in it, but it's about Derek's case… *Murder Story* was about the evil of capital punishment, which Ludovic Kennedy calls 'legal killing'.

Source E: *The New York Times*, 21 October, 2009.

British Journalist, Ludovic Kennedy, Dies at 89
Mr. Kennedy's fights against injustice began with the case of Derek Bentley, who was hanged in 1953 for the murder of a constable during a burglary… Despite wide protests, it took 40 years to officially exonerate him. Mr. Kennedy wrote a play about the case, 'Murder Story'.

His 1961 book, 'Ten Rillington Place', re-examined the conviction of Timothy Evans, a retarded man hanged in 1950 for the murder of his wife and baby… The Bentley and Evans cases were among several that led to the abolition of capital punishment in Britain in 1965.

Source F: *Crime, Punishment and Protest*, Allan Todd, 2002.

Changing attitudes
Cases like Derek Bentley's made people focus more clearly on the way in which the death penalty was imposed. Some newspapers commented that the whole system of reprieves by the Home Secretary had become a lottery. Some criminals were sentenced to 10–15 years in prison, while others who had committed the same offence were hanged. Many questioned the fairness of the system. Many prison governors and prison officers also began to change their views about the death penalty.

Pressure groups were also important in changing attitudes. Amnesty International for example often organised petitions for reprieves.

Source G: From public opinion surveys carried out by Mass Observation. People were asked if they were in favour of suspending capital punishment.

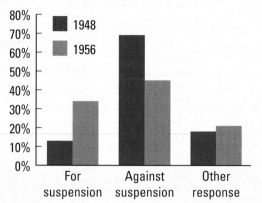

Source: Mass Observation Survey data, 1956.

Source H: From Mass Observation public opinion survey, 1956. People who had recently made up their minds against capital punishment were asked which, if any, of the following had influenced their decision. The chart below shows their responses.

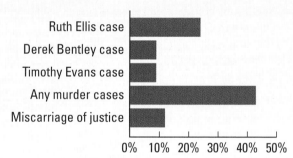

Source: Mass Observation Survey data, 1956.

Source I: From the Spartacus Educational website. A history of the work of the Labour politician, Sydney Silverman.

Silverman was a strong opponent of capital punishment and in 1948 managed to persuade the House of Commons to agree to a five-year suspension of executions. However, this clause in the Criminal Justice Bill was defeated in the House of Lords. As a result Silverman founded the Campaign for the Abolition of the Death Penalty. In 1953 he published his book, *Hanged and Innocent?*

Source: www.spartacus.schoolnet.co.uk.

Follow up more leads

At this stage in your enquiry, you will have a number of leads organised as key issues. You now need to follow them up, using the source file and any other useful sources you have found. Look back at page 44 to keep yourself on track. Review your material – can you identify any gaps which you need to research? What are the key areas that you should go into in more depth?

Review and organise material – reach conclusions

Finally, you will need to reach a conclusion. In this example you should decide what the importance of the Derek Bentley case was. You could summarise your key points in a concept map and draw arrows to show how the factors link. For example, public outrage over the hanging of a young man with the mental age of an 11-year old encouraged campaigners, who in turn pressured Parliament to change the law.

You have discovered that Derek's Bentley's case did not bring about the ending of the death penalty by itself. Many people had doubts before the case. Note, too, that a majority of the British public still supported the death penalty in 1956 (Source G). The task for the enquiry is to show how important the case was – if it increased public concern, strengthened the campaigns and combined with other factors to help make Parliament more willing to suspend the death penalty.

Present your conclusions

This activity gives you practice in presenting the conclusion of your controlled assessment task. After you have completed the activity you could turn to Maximise your marks on page 71 to see if your answer could be improved.

Activities

12. Make a set of notes to go with your concept map. Use the same headings. Do not use more than two sides of paper. You can include quotations from your sources in your notes. Try to use them in your answer, but make sure you explain why they are important and include the name of your source.

13. Write up your enquiry: What was the importance of the case of Derek Bentley in the campaigns to end the death penalty in England?

Following up an enquiry 2: Changes in the policing of protest – compare police methods in the Cable Street Riots, 1936 and the Miners' Strike, 1984

This practice enquiry is different from enquiry 1. Enquiry 1 asked you to find out why the case of Derek Bentley was important. This enquiry gives you practice in making comparisons and deciding how much policing changed.

You want to find out whether the police methods were different in the way they handled the law and order problems they faced in 1936 and 1984. Follow the enquiry stages outlined on page 44: identify your sources; sift and sort your information; follow up your leads.

Begin by using pages 23–24 of this book. Then go on to the information given in the source file on pages 51–52. You can then follow up more leads if you like. Video footage of Cable Street and the Miners' Strike can be found on YouTube. You can also go to www.pearsonhotlinks.co.uk, insert the express code 6466P and then click on 'Cable Street Riots, 1936' or 'Miners' Strike, 1984'.

When you follow up your leads, don't forget to stick to the enquiry stages shown in the diagram on page 44, which you followed in enquiry 1. When looking at sources, remember the RDR tests (see page 46). You will find accounts from plenty of eyewitnesses, but many of them will be very angry about the events they saw. This may affect the reliability of what they say. Also many people's opinions were influenced by their political beliefs. For example, Tony Benn (Source G) was a leading Labour politician. He opposed the Conservative prime minister, Margaret Thatcher, and her views about how the police should handle the Miners' Strike. Can you tell from Source G that Tony Benn was sympathetic to the striking miners?

Activities

Making and sorting notes

14. Read pages 23–24 and the source file. Make a bullet point list of useful information, for example:

Cable street, 1936
- 250,000 people assembled to prevent Oswald Mosley's Blackshirts from marching through the East End of London.

Miners' Strike, 1984
- Police set up roadblocks to prevent 'flying pickets'.

15. Begin to organise your notes. For each protest, arrange them into a chart like the one below. Notes on Cable Street have been started for you. Add details to each bullet point and add new bullet points.

Cable Street, 1936

Police aims:
- to allow the BUF to march
- to keep the streets clear
- to keep protestors apart in order to prevent violence

Police problems:
- narrow streets
- barricades built by anti-fascists

Police methods:
- planning and organisation
- uniform and equipment
- tactics

Miners' Strike 1984
-

16. Now colour-code your chart. Use green when police methods were similar and red for different methods.

17. Finally, think about how much change you can see.

Source file

Source A: *People in Change*, Josh Brooman, 1994.

From the start, meetings of the BUF often led to fighting between black-shirted Fascists and left-wing groups such as the Communist Party. From 1935 onwards there was a great deal of fighting in London's East End, where the Fascists held marches and rallies to intimidate the Jewish population. The worst fighting took place on Sunday, 4 October 1936 when Communists, Jewish groups and [other groups opposed to the Fascists] decided to halt a Fascist march through the East End. In the 'Battle of Cable Street' that day, 70 people were injured in street fighting.

Source B: The *Daily Worker* newspaper, 5 October, 1936.

Many of the side-streets...were cordoned off by police long before the march was due to start. No one was allowed to go through unless he could satisfy the cordon officer that he had legitimate business there. The inhabitants were scarcely permitted to leave these streets at all...The police called every modern device into action to help them in their activities.

Source C: *The Battle of Cable Street: Myths and Realities*, Richard Price and Martin Sullivan, 1994.

The fascists were due to gather in Royal Mint Street at 2.30pm [in order to march into nearby Cable Street]. Hours beforehand every street around was thronged with people. Up to 300,000 anti-fascists had assembled. Ten thousand police, according to the Daily Herald's estimate, were brought in from all over London and deployed to protect the fascist march in what was obviously a well-prepared battle-plan.

Fascists formed a column of 3,000 stretching for half a mile. The Blackshirts jeered back at distant booing. They chanted 'we want Mosley' [leader of the BUF], to which the crowd shouted back, 'So do we, dead or alive'. Police attempted to clear the streets close to Royal Mint Street with repeated baton charges. Anti-fascist protestors responded with stones, fireworks and marbles hurled under horses' hooves chanting 'They shall not pass!'.

Mosley finally appeared around 3.40pm. Shortly before this, the police had begun preparing to clear a route for the BUF march. But by the time Mosley spoke to the Police Commissioner these plans had been abandoned and Mosley was told that the march could not proceed because of the threat of disorder.

Source D: Pickets at Orgreave running from a police charge, 18 June 1984. The police are aiming to clear the road so that lorries containing coke (fuel made from coal) can leave the depot.

Source E: From the *Guardian* newspaper, 5 October 1936.

Fascist march stopped after disorderly scenes

The Communists and Independent Labour Party had arranged a counter-demonstration... So great were the crowds that had assembled for this purpose...that all the traffic was held up. Every time a bus or tram load of policemen arrived they were greeted with...booing and the Communist salute.

The police experienced great difficulty in clearing the roadway, and both mounted and foot police used their truncheons. There were several arrests, and the pressure of the crowds on the pavements broke a number of shop windows...

Stones and other missiles were thrown and a bag of pepper was burst in front of [a] policeman's horse.

In Cable Street a crowd seized materials from a builder's yard and began to construct a barricade. They used corrugated iron, barrels, coal, and glass to construct a barrier, even pulling up paving-stones. When the police intervened they were greeted with a shower of stones, and reinforcements had to be sent and a charge made before order could be restored and the barricade removed.

Source F: From a speech by the Prime Minister, Margaret Thatcher, on 30 May, 1984. She is speaking about the mass picket by striking miners at Orgreave.

What we have got is an attempt to substitute the rule of the mob for the rule of law. It must not succeed. The miners are using violence and intimidation to impose their will on others who do not want it... The rule of law must prevail over the rule of the mob.

Source G: From Tony Benn's diaries, published in 1994. This is part of his account of 31 May 1984.

Over the last few days there have been terrible scenes outside the Orgreave Coke Depot, where 7,000 pickets have been attacked by mounted and foot police with riot shields and helmets. It looks like a civil war. You see the police charging with big staves and police dogs chasing miners across fields, then miners respond by throwing stones and trying to drag a telegraph pole across a road; there are burning buildings and road blocks.

Writing up your answer

The moderator will be looking for four main things – that you have:

- kept your answer focused on the enquiry
- found information from different sources
- backed up your statements with information
- communicated your answer by organising it well and using good spelling, punctuation and grammar.

The activities which follow will help you to improve your writing. Remember to use the skills you have learned when you write up your controlled assessment answer.

Activities

Improving writing

18. Imagine you are the moderator. Study example extracts 1 and 2 on page 53 and discuss with a partner the good and bad points (you will find the answers at the bottom of page 53).

19. Improve examples 1 and 2. You can use bullet points.

20. Study example extract 3. It is part of a high-level response. It compares police methods, finding similarities and differences, and giving details. Add examples to support the last statement in paragraphs two and three.

Compare police methods in the Cable Street Riots, 1936 and the Miners' Strike, 1984

Example extract 1

They were much the same. In both people blocked the roads and threw stones at police, the police used horses and hundreds of policemen and the police charged and people ran away from them.

Example extract 2

The Battle of Cable Street was a political protest against the Fascists in Britain. In October 1936, there was violence because the Blackshirts wanted to march against the Jews in London and the anti-Fascists were determined to stop them from going along Cable Street. The police aimed to protect the marchers because the march was legal. In the end the anti-Fascists won and the march was stopped, but a lot of people were injured. The Miners' Strike was different; it was not a political protest. But the miners used mass pickets to try to stop other miners going to work and coal being moved. The police aimed to protect the working miners and the lorry drivers. The biggest demonstrations were at Orgreave. This was similar to Cable Street because there was violence and injury there. But the pickets did not succeed. Lorries did still transport coal. So they were different because in Cable Street the police did not achieve their main aim and they did in the Miners' Strike.

Example extract 3

One police method in October 1936 was careful planning. The police planned how to deal with a huge law and order problem. Violence was expected because the Blackshirts wanted to march against the Jews in London and the anti-Fascists were determined to stop them from going along Cable Street. The police aimed to protect the marchers and keep the streets clear because the march was legal. Police planning included bringing in thousands of police from all over London (according to the Daily Herald) to reinforce the local police. The Daily Worker gives us evidence that the police controlled the streets hours before the march...

Police planning in the Miners' Strike was similar, although the strike was on a bigger scale – covering huge areas of the country and lasting for over a year. Firstly they controlled the movement of pickets, stopping them leaving their counties; secondly police were brought in from other areas. But there were also differences. Non-local police were used in mining areas not just to reinforce locals, but also because 'local police might be sympathetic to the miners' [answer then gives examples, quoting sources].

There were also similarities in the methods used to remove barricades and road blocks [answer details similarities in the use of mounted police, mass police charges, and batons]. But some of the biggest changes were in police communications and equipment between 1936 and 1984...

Summary

Success in your enquiry comes from:

- sticking to the focus of the enquiry
- using a range of sources, keeping their relevance and reliability in mind
- organising your answer to show good quality of written communication.

Example 2 has more detail and has made some comments about similarity and difference. But the student has side-tracked. The answer is mainly about the reason for the protests. There is not enough about police methods. Example 2 does not refer to any sources.

Example 1 does identify similarities, but it is not detailed enough and it does not identify any differences. It does not refer to any sources.

Part B Representations of history

Was Victorian policing effective *c.*1880–*c.*1901?

54

Learning outcomes

By the end of this topic, you should be able to:

- describe some of the strengths and weaknesses of the police service *c.*1880–*c.*1901
- understand that people have different views about the effectiveness of police forces in late Victorian England
- understand why there are differing views about the effectiveness of the police.

In Part B of your Controlled Assessment you are exploring different ideas about Victorian policing. People at the time had different views about the police, just as we do today. The aim of this chapter is to explore this issue and understand why historians' views about the police also differ.

Activities

1. In groups, list examples of different types of police work shown on the news, in television programmes, in newspapers and in films.

2. Now group your list into examples which you think a) show the police being effective and b) show the police not being effective.

3. Looking at your two lists, now try to give (a) five words (adjectives) to describe the police being effective, for example 'efficient' and (b) five words (adjectives) to describe the police not being effective, for example 'violent'.

4. Study Source A. What impression of the policeman has the artist created? Does the policeman seem threatening or trustworthy? Think about: his uniform, appearance, expression, lack of visible weapon. What can you learn from Source A about public attitudes to the police in 1901?

Source A: The policeman', from a set of postcards titled 'Familiar Figures of London', published in 1901.

The Victorian police force

When police forces were set up in the first half of the nineteenth century, they were unpopular. People:

- criticised them for violent and drunken behaviour
- resented the cost of running a police force
- feared them as a threat to their personal and political freedom.

By 1880, attitudes to the police had changed. Reforms meant there was less drunkenness in the police force, for example. The policeman was generally seen more as a friend than a threat (except, of course, by criminals!) The cost of running police forces seemed worth it to most people.

A golden age?

Late Victorian England is described by some historians as a 'golden age' of policing because of the amount of public trust and approval. Greater distrust of the police emerged again later in the twentieth century.

But historians also ask whether this really was a 'golden age'. They have come to different conclusions about three areas: preventing crime, solving crime and dealing with large protests.

The police and crime prevention

The evidence about this issue is questionable. When historians do not have enough evidence or enough reliable evidence, this leads to different views about how effective the police were at reducing the crime rate.

Crime statistics are difficult for us to use as evidence about whether crime is going up or down. For example, a higher number of convictions might not mean more crime is actually occurring.

- If police detection of crime improved, then the number of convictions might be evidence of better police work rather than evidence of more crime.

- New crimes were added to the law in the period 1880–1990. For example, after education became compulsory, parents whose children did not attend school were fined; motorists were fined when new road traffic offences were created after cars came into use. Convictions under these new laws could increase the crime figures but this would not be evidence that crime had increased.

The way crimes are recorded is also important. You can see from Source D that records were not the same in all police forces. Crime rates do seem to have gone down at the end of the nineteenth century. That suggests some criminals may have been deterred because they felt it was more likely that they might be caught. It is difficult to prove this and historians are careful about the conclusions they draw from the evidence of statistics, as you can see from Source E on page 56. Overall, this historian's conclusion is that there was an improvement: that the crime trend was 'downwards'. This might suggest that police had some success in crime prevention. What is the view of the cartoonist in Source F (page 56)?

Source B: *English Police*, Clive Emsley, 1996.

Except in moments of **moral panic** such as... the Jack the Ripper murders of 1888, criticism of the English police... brought squeals of protest and complaints that such criticism was unhelpful [for law and order].

Moral panic: a short time when the public is full of panic, thinking that a group or individual is a threat to society.

Source C: *Crime and Justice 1750–1950*, B. Godfrey and P. Lawrence, 2005.

By the final quarter of the nineteenth century, both the idea and experience of policing had undergone a dramatic change. What has subsequently been popularly perceived as a 'golden age' of policing had begun.

Source D: From a report by a government committee on criminal statistics in 1895. The committee is reporting on problems in the police tables of crimes and convictions which were published each year.

The figures have been prepared by the police with great care, but some forces have proceeded on one basis and others on another. The making of an attendance order [when a parent failed to send a child to school] was treated as a conviction by 121 police forces and excluded from the returns by 27. This alone added about 20,000 convictions a year to the tables, where there was in fact no conviction.

Source E: *Crime and Criminals of Victorian London*, Adrian Gray, 2006.

> There has been much debate among historians as to whether crime worsened during the Victorian period. Statistics are problematic. There were variations in statistical collection and an improving police force could lead to more arrests. Some activities became illegal that were not before as the State became more regulatory [made new laws to protect citizens]. However despite the occasional scare, there is general consensus that the crime trend in Victorian England was downwards.

Catching criminals

Catching the criminal after a crime was the work of the detective branch. In London, the detective force grew from 216 in 1878 to 294 in 1883 and their number of arrests grew from 13,000 to 18,000. Police forces throughout the country began to improve their detective branches in the 1880s. The main improvements were:

- Better record keeping – criminal records were kept which included descriptions and photographs. This meant that more **habitual criminals** were caught.

- Improved systems for classifying information – the Bertillon system (Source G) recorded details on thousands of cards. It was used in the 1890s but without much success. It was difficult to use before the invention of computers could sort data more efficiently. It was mainly replaced by fingerprint records after 1901 (see page 39). But Bertillon's system of taking photographs of criminals in a standard way is still used today.

- Using new technology – photographic techniques improved during the years 1880–1901. Details of crime scenes as well as criminals were recorded. Bertillon's high-level camera (Source G) gave a more precise picture of crime scenes. Better telephone networks in the 1890s allowed faster communication.

Activities

5. Study Source E. Why does the historian say 'statistics are problematic'? Find three reasons.

6. Study Source F. It shows a policeman on his **beat**. How does the cartoonist suggest that the police were not effective in preventing crime?

7. Can you find evidence in Source F which also suggests that the police might deter criminals?

Source F: A cartoon published in *Punch* magazine in 1888.

WHITECHAPEL, 1888.

Member of "Criminal Class." "FINE BODY O' MEN, THE PER-LEECE!"
Ditto. "UNCOMMON FINE!—IT'S LUCKY FOR HUS AS THERE'S SECH A BLOOMIN' FEW ON 'EM!!!

Beat: the set route a police constable patrolled. He was expected to average about 2.5 miles per hour.

Habitual criminals: people who often commit crimes.

Identifiers: ways of proving a criminal's identity by recording their photographs and five key measurements such as head length and middle-finger length.

Source G: A photograph by Alphonse Bertillon showing his methods of identifying criminals, 1893. Alphonse Bertillon used photography and measurement to create a record of unique **identifiers** that could be used to track suspects.

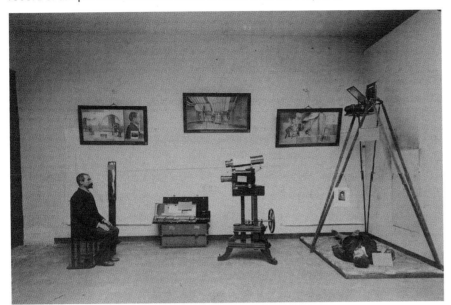

Source H: *The English Police*, Clive Emsley, 1996

In general, detective policing was not regarded as a priority among the chief constables, and training for the tasks, when there was any, remained rudimentary [very basic].

However, in spite of the new technology, detectives could not do much to catch offenders unless there were witnesses who would give good descriptions of them. During the Whitechapel murders scare of 1888, the public was angry because the police couldn't track Jack the Ripper down. It is unfair to judge the success of police detection just by the public reaction to the Jack the Ripper case. But during the nineteenth century, forces hadn't had the training (Source H) or the technical aids to solve crimes. Fingerprint evidence was a breakthrough, but that only developed at the end of the period (page 39). We can see that detective work improved during the period, but that faster progress was not possible before scientific and technical advances in the twentieth century.

Policing demonstrations: keeping order or threat to liberty?

Although public approval of the police grew in the nineteenth century, many people were still worried about the role of the police in dealing with public protests. Did police controls threaten people's freedom to protest to the government? The police had a duty to maintain order and prevent riot. Citizens had the right to gather to make peaceful protests. This meant that police leaders had difficult decisions to make about what action to take when a protest was planned. The case study on pages 58–59 shows this.

Activities

Did detectives become better at catching criminals?

Yes   No

8. Make a large copy of the two hands – or create two columns headed 'On the one hand' and 'On the other hand'.

9. Sort the points below into two 'hands'. You can also add points and more information of your own.

   - more detectives
   - little training of detectives
   - Bertillon system difficult to use
   - greater number of arrests
   - press and public criticism, especially in the case of the Whitechapel murders, 1888
   - new technology
   - better record keeping
   - technical improvements not widely used.

Case study: the Trafalgar Square Riots, 1887

In the years 1886–87 there were many mass demonstrations by the hungry and unemployed. In London they gathered in Trafalgar Square.

After Black Monday (see Fact file) a new Commissioner of Police was appointed to lead the London Metropolitan Police Force. Sir Charles Warren was an ex-soldier. He was expected to be good at improving police discipline and training them to deal with large protests.

When a protest about unemployment was planned for Sunday 13 November, 1887, Warren banned the meeting and decided to use force against anyone who disobeyed the ban. The leaders of the demonstration went ahead with the protest. Over 70,000 people marched on Trafalgar Square (see Fact file).

Warren deployed 4,000 policemen on foot, together with policemen on horses. He also had reinforcements from the army – 200 mounted and armed life guards and about 800 armed grenadier guards on foot. Violent clashes between the protestors and the police followed (Source I). Warren, on horseback, calmly directed police operations. The demonstration was broken up and 300 people were arrested.

Did Warren use too much force? Was it an attack on people's right to protest? Was he defending Londoners from the threat of riot and damage? He was criticised by some and praised by others. What do Sources I and J suggest? Historians also have different views. Nowadays the same issue still exists, for example there were criticisms of the role of the police at the G20 summit in London Docklands in 2009.

Fact file
Black Monday, 1886

Rioting and looting took place after a protest meeting in Trafalgar Square on Monday 8 February, 1886.

281 businesses claimed compensation for riot damage – about £50,000 (£25 million in today's money).

The police were strongly criticised for not preventing the damage and looting. The head of the London Metropolitan Police Force, Commissioner Henderson, had to resign.

Source J: From *The Times* newspaper, 14 November, 1887.

He has earned the thanks of the country for his defence of public liberty. Thanks to his masterly arrangements and the way they were carried out by the force under his control, the attempt to put London at the mercy of a ruffianly mob was totally defeated.

Source I: From the newspaper, *Graphic*, 19 November, 1887.
The drawing illustrated an article titled 'The Riot in Trafalgar Square'.

Activities

Create your tug of war team!

Defence of property   Threat to liberty

10. A tug of war team needs to be strong and well linked, so that it pulls well. Create your 'teams' by adding points which give strength to each 'side'. Complete each of the following sentences using the 'strengthening points' below. Link the argument together choosing from the 'linking words' or by using linking words of your own. There is extra information in the Fact file, which you can use if you wish.

- Warren's actions can be seen as effective policing because…
- Warren's actions can be seen as bad policing because…

Strengthening points

- The police violence and use of armed soldiers was a brutal attack on peaceful marchers.
- British citizens in the nineteenth century had the right to protest peacefully.
- Criminals and looters used the large demonstrations to cover their activities.
- The police had a duty to protect people and property from damage and looting.
- After November 1887, demonstrations were orderly; the frequent rioting in London died down.
- The marchers defied a police ban.
- There were doubts at the time about whether the police ban on the march was legal.
- Firm police action was necessary to stop the possibility of serious disorder.

Linking words

Also…; Additionally…; Furthermore…; Because…

11. Decide which argument is stronger overall and give your reasons.

12. Take a vote with other members of your class. You could also hold a class debate.

13. Write a paragraph to explain why there are different views of Bloody Sunday (13 November, 1887).

14. Make a summary of the strengths and weaknesses of policing *c.*1880–1901. Include examples from all three key aspects of policing: (a) crime prevention (b) crime detection and (c) policing protest.

Fact file
Bloody Sunday, 1887

Complaints to the police from the public and press grew during the autumn of 1887. They were concerned about the disorder which accompanied frequent protest meetings in Trafalgar Square.

One group of marchers was led by an MP, R. Cunninghame Graham. Other well-known figures included: Annie Besant, a leading campaigner for workers' rights; George Bernard Shaw, the playwright; William Morris, the artist, and John Burns, a trade union leader.

The home secretary (the government minister responsible for the police) did not back Warren's decision to ban the march.

One protestor, Alfred Linell, was badly injured by a police horse. He died later in hospital.

Peaceful meetings continued to be held with police permission in Hyde Park – in a large, open space where damage to property was less likely.

Britain's economy improved after 1887 and there was less unemployment.

Summary

- Public approval of the police was generally high in the years 1880–1901, except in times of moral panic.
- Historians have different views about the effectiveness of Victorian policing.
- This is because the evidence is problematic or points in different directions.

Understanding and analysing representations of history

Learning outcomes

By the end of this topic, you should be able to:

- understand what is meant by representations of history
- understand how historical representations are created
- analyse representations and judge how far they differ from one another.

What are representations of history?

A representation of history is a depiction of the past created visually or in words. It is designed to create an image of things in the past – an event, a movement, the role of an individual and so on. Historians create representations when they write about the past. They create a picture of what life was like, why people acted as they did and what the consequences of events and developments were. Novelists, filmmakers and cartoonists also give us an image of past societies and events. In each case, the way they show their subject creates a representation of it.

Analysing representations

Someone who creates a representation takes some of the same steps you might take when creating a Facebook entry or taking a photograph. You choose what you are taking a photograph of or how to show yourself. Do you want to record an important event? Will you show it as happy or solemn? Do you want to show the beauty of a particular place? To get the effect you want, you choose which things to focus on. Sometimes you decide to leave things out. You make decisions about how to show the scene or the event.

When you analyse a representation you should look at each part separately and think about how it affects the overall image. From the details you can infer (work out) what impression the artist or author is trying to give.

A modern example of a representation

Let's first take a modern image and use the same skills needed to analyse a historical representation. Study Source A.

Source A: An illustration from the website of the British Tourist board, 2009. It shows a scene on the east coast of England.

Inclusion of the boat and the windmill

Blue sky: would the photograph have been taken on a rainy day?

Uncrowded scene: no objects in the centre of the picture

Happy-looking young couple: do people look happy all the time? Why has the photographer not shown just one person alone?

Note the details the photographer has chosen to include. Why have these details been included? What messages are they designed to give? Can you suggest anything which may have been deliberately left out? What do you think is the purpose of the representation in Source A?

Now study Source B. It is a photograph taken in the middle of an August morning. It shows a part of the coast near to the place shown in Source A. The building in the background is a nuclear power station.

Source B: A holiday photograph taken at Sizewell on the Suffolk coast, August 2009.

What parts of Source A are supported by details in Source B? Would you use Source B to advertise holidays on the Suffolk coast? If not, why not? If yes, what parts of the photograph would you select?

Source A is not *inaccurate*, but Source B helps to show us that Source A is not a *complete* representation. Source A is one view and, when we analyse it, we can infer the message and purpose of this representation from the choices the photographer has made. Source A is designed to portray the coast as attractive and uncrowded, a place to enjoy walks and be happy. Its purpose is to encourage people to take holidays in the area.

Activities

1. Describe the representation of the east coast of England given in Source A. Use details from Source A. You could begin 'Source A is a representation of the east coast. It is designed to portray it as… We can tell this because…'

2. Try to use most of the following words and phrases in your description (you can use them in any order):

   - selected
   - chosen to
   - omitted
   - deliberately
   - highlighted
   - included
   - incomplete.

   You can also use details from Source B if you wish.

A case study in historical representations: the police and the Whitechapel murders of 1888

The historical context

From 31 August to 9 November 1888, a series of five gruesome murders took place in Whitechapel in the East End of London. The killer was labelled 'Jack the Ripper' by the newspapers. He stabbed his female victims and cut out parts of their body. Mary Kelly, thought to be at least victim number five, was particularly badly mutilated in November (see Source C). Fear of when the murderer would strike again caused increasing panic in the autumn of 1888. There was much criticism of the police for failing to catch him. The Ripper case became so notorious that details of the murders and criticisms of the police were even published in the USA (see Source D). Other murders before and after these may also have been the work of the same killer. You can find out more at www.pearsonhotlinks.co.uk: insert the express code 6466P and then click on 'Whitechapel murders, 1888'.

Analysing artists' representations

Source E was published by Punch Magazine in England in September 1888. Cartoonists often use part of an image to represent something. The policeman is a symbol for the whole police force. We can analyse this cartoon to show that the artist has created a representation which is highly critical of the London Metropolitan Police force.

The analysis shows that overall the cartoon is a representation of the police force in 1888 which gives an impression that the force is ineffective. The police are unable even to see how to find the killer in the Whitechapel murders or to deal with ordinary criminals.

Source C: Extract from the post mortem report on the body of Mary Kelly by Dr Thomas Bond. The report went on to describe further mutilations to the body.

> The face was gashed in all directions, the nose, cheeks, eyebrows and ears being partly removed. The heart was removed…

Source D: From an article entitled 'Whitechapel startled by a fourth murder', *New York Times*, 9 September 1888.

> …the detectives have no clue. The London police and detective force is probably the stupidest in the world.

Source E: A cartoon published by *Punch* magazine in 1888. Blind Man's Buff was a game played by children.

The policeman is shown blindfolded, and is helpless because he cannot see where to go.

Criminal-looking figures are ducking so the policeman cannot catch them.

BLIND-MAN'S BUFF.
(As played by the Police.)
" TURN ROUND THREE TIMES,
AND CATCH WHOM YOU MAY ! "

The caption likens police action to a game of 'catch who you can'.

Expressions on faces show a lack of respect for the policeman.

The poster indicates there are murders to be solved.

Source F: From a popular newspaper, *The Illustrated Police News*, published in 1888.

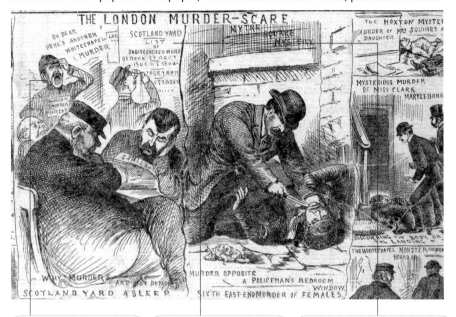

The policeman saying 'oh dear...' is shown as helpless. How does the drawing do that?

Policemen are shown as being asleep while the murder takes place.

The artist has chosen to include a poster with a list of 'undiscovered' (meaning unsolved) murderers.

Analysing written historical representations

To analyse written representations, you can use the same skills you have already developed to analyse visual sources. You should still note what the author has chosen to focus on, what he or she has chosen to include, what has been omitted and how words are used to build up an impression.

Source G: From a local newspaper, the *East London Advertiser*, 15 September, 1888.

It is clear that the Detective Department at Scotland Yard is in an utterly hopeless and worthless condition; if there were a capable Director of Criminal Investigations, the scandalous exhibition of police stupidity and ineptitude [ineffectiveness or uselessness] revealed at the East End inquests, and the immunity [freedom from arrest] enjoyed by criminals murder after murder would not have angered and disgusted the public feeling as it has done.

Analysing the views of historians

The views of historians are also representations. Historians writing about any society have to make choices. They choose what to concentrate on. They also come to views about the topics they research. Using the evidence, they make judgements about the role of individuals or the reasons for an event, and so on. In their writing they give their views. Sometimes historians' views differ.

But we cannot think about historians' writing in quite the same way as Sources F and G. Unlike representations such as Sources F and G, historians aim to create an accurate representation of the past that they have researched. The views of historians may differ because they're looking at or looking for different things, or because they interpret the evidence differently.

Source H: *Jack the Ripper: The Definitive History,* Paul Begg, 2005.

> The Whitechapel Murders focused attention on the deficiencies and inadequacies of the police. The importance of the crimes was that they exposed the police to widespread criticism.

Source I: From *Crime and Justice 1750–1950,* written by Barry Godfrey and Paul Lawrence, 2005.

> What do these isolated cases [the murders in Whitechapel in 1888] really tell us about homicide in the Victorian period? Should we not look at the typical or general picture? Was murder an extraordinary or a common feature of everyday life? In the Victorian period, despite the stories of Jack the Ripper, murder was not common and society was not as violent as it is often portrayed. At least that is what the statistics suggest.

Activity

9. Study Sources H and I. They are written by historians. Which of the following statements are correct? You can choose as many as you like. (The answer is at the bottom of the page.)

- The historians disagree.
- The historians do not actually disagree.
- The historians are writing about different things.
- The historians have different views about the importance of the Whitechapel murders.
- Both historians' views of the importance of Whitechapel murders are accurate.

The differences between Sources H and I are explained by what the historians are looking at. Begg is concentrating on a short period of time; Godfrey and Lawrence are looking at patterns over 200 years. Moreover, Begg is looking at attitudes to the police while Godfrey and Lawrence are looking at crimes. Although they are different, both can be accurate in their views. Just as when people in a house look out of different windows, or look into the distance or close to the house, their different *focus* will give them a different view of the scenery. It will be important to keep this idea of *focus* in mind when you look at differences in the representations of historians. Historians are not usually wrong or inaccurate when they differ, but they may have looked at the topic from a different perspective.

Answer: all statements except the first one are correct. The views are different, but they are not actually disagreeing with one another.

Comparing representations

Sources J and K are both representations of the Commissioner of the Metropolitan Police, Sir Charles Warren. How far do they differ? To find out, follow these three steps.

1. Analyse each source. When analysing representations, first identify the big points. Historians usually make a big point – their main conclusion or view – and they use detailed points of evidence to back it up. In Sources J and K, the main points have been highlighted.

2. Compare them. Draw a table like the one which has been started on page 66, so you can compare the sources carefully. In the first column put specific points you want to check. In the second column add anything from the other source which supports or challenges this point. Use the third column to make notes on what you have found.

3. Reach a conclusion about 'how far'. Decide how much the differences you have found actually matter. Are they small differences, such as a matter of detail, or big differences about the main points of the representation? How much agreement is there? Weigh up the similarities and differences to decide how far they differ.

Source J: *Jack the Ripper: The Definitive History*, Paul Begg, 2005.

So strong is the view that Warren was a lousy commissioner, that it is difficult to buck the trend [challenge this view].

However history *has* dealt unfairly with Warren who was the right man for the right job at the wrong time. He faced a press intolerant of mistakes. Nobody could have emerged unscathed [undamaged].

At first [in 1886] Warren's appointment was greeted with satisfaction. Warren's skills were right for the job, as *The Times* observed: 'Sir Charles Warren is precisely the man whom sensible London would have chosen to preside over the Police Force of the Metropolis [London]. What this meant was that it was generally believed that the police lacked discipline and needed a firm hand in control. Warren was selected and was generally thought to be an excellent person for the job.

Source: The Times, *1886.*

Source K: From *Critical Years at the Yard*, Belton Cobb, 1956.

… Sir Charles Warren [was] an autocratic, elderly soldier who wanted to run everything in his own way – the military way. He was inclined moreover to regard his fellow men (or at any rate the civilians amongst them) as fools…

On the night of September 8th, 1888 Annie Chapman was murdered in a street in Whitechapel. As had happened in the other murders, the body was horribly ripped and mutilated…

The third in the series of murders committed by 'Jack the Ripper' brought public excitement to a high pitch. It seemed as if the most devilish murderer of all time was at large in London. No one knew when he would strike next – but everyone was sure he would strike again…

The Police were extremely active… as there were no reliable clues of any sort to the identity of the murderer, the best chance seemed to be to catch him red-handed when he tried to strike again. That could only be done by increasing the patrols in the Whitechapel streets – so, 'Sir Charles Warren sent every available man into the East End'.

Meanwhile, the C.I.D. followed up everything that showed the slightest sign of leading towards a clue…

The newspapers were extremely critical of the way the enquiries were being conducted. As each fresh murder was announced, every morning paper and every evening paper devoted a whole page or more of its space to the account of it… Sir Charles Warren – 'this hopeless … failure' – was assailed, partly because he was a soldier playing the part of a policeman.

Activities

Create a table like the one below.

10. Identify points you want to check in Source J. Remember that you are looking at how Warren is portrayed. You could enter big points in red and smaller details in black.

11. Check Source K to see what is said about these points – are they confirmed, challenged or just not mentioned?

12. Now repeat, starting with Source K and look for any extra points you've so far not compared.

13. Weigh up the differences and write your conclusion. Include these key phrases (delete the words which do not fit your conclusion):

- There are *some/many* points on which Begg and Cobb agree…
- However there are *small/major* differences in the way they portray Warren…
- Overall they are mainly *in agreement/differ* to a large extent in their representations of Warren…

Points in Source J	Points in Source K	My notes
History has been unfair to Warren. There is a strong view that he was a 'lousy' commissioner.	He was criticised as a hopeless failure, partly because he was a soldier playing at the part of a policeman.	Source J is sympathetic to Warren. Source K is not. Source K doesn't directly say he was a hopeless failure, but because he includes the criticism and doesn't challenge it, it suggests he is critical of Warren. 'Because he was a soldier playing the part of a policeman' are Cobb's own words. That suggests he thinks Warren was a poor commissioner.
Warren was the right man for the job.	Warren was a soldier who wanted to run everything his own way. He was a soldier playing the part of a policeman.	Cobb seems to be criticising Warren's character and he also seems to think a soldier was not right for the job.
Warren was in the job at the wrong time. The press were intolerant. Nobody could have emerged unscathed.	The newspapers were extremely critical…	
	The police were extremely active. Warren sent every available man into the East End.	

Summary

- Representations are created to give an impression of an aspect of the past.
- The impression is created by what is included and by the way details are drawn or by the words used.
- Historians' interpretations are also representations the past. They sometimes differ because of the particular historian's focus.

Evaluating representations

When you are evaluating a representation, you are deciding how good it is. When you evaluate anything in everyday life – what clothes to buy, for example – you use criteria. Does it fit? Is it in fashion? Is it too expensive? Is the colour right for me? You also make some criteria more important than others. If something doesn't fit, you won't buy it, even if the colour is right!

You will also use criteria when you weigh up representations of history. But let's work on an everyday example first, and then you can apply your skills to evaluating historical representations.

Using criteria to evaluate representations of history

There are many different kinds of representation. You could be judging between an extract from a history book, a cartoon, a work of historical fiction or a film portrayal of an event in the past. Apply criteria to each of them to make your judgement. But remember, in order to weigh up a historical representation you must first have good knowledge of the issue which is represented.

Using your knowledge, you can apply these tests to a representation:

- Is it **accurate**? Test the representation against what you know. Is it correct?

- Is it **complete**? Does your knowledge suggest important aspects are missing?

- Is it **objective**? Analyse the representation to see whether it is fair or unbalanced in its treatment. Here you could also think about the purpose of the author or artist.

For example, what overall rating (1–5) would you give to Source A on page 68? It is a representation of policing by the London Metropolitan Police while Sir Charles Warren was in charge from 1886 to 1888. First study the context box. Then follow the steps in Activities 3, 4 and 5 to help you reach your judgement.

Activities

1. Identify three criteria you use when you decide what to eat. Compare them with a partner.
2. With a partner pick a film or TV drama you have both seen.
   a. Choose three criteria by which to evaluate it, for example 'funny' or 'action-packed'.
   b. Give it a rating of 1–3 against each of the criteria, and discuss your rating with your partner. You do not need to agree, but you should each be able to back up the rating you give. Refer specifically to the film or drama.
   c. Give the programme or film an overall star rating of 1–5. Make a display to explain your overall evaluation to your class, making sure you refer to the criteria you have used. Was one criterion so important that it had the most influence on your overall rating?

Activities

3. Draw up a table with three columns headed: 'How accurate?', 'How complete?' 'How objective?'
4. Fill in your three columns for Source A on page 68. You can use points given in the context box and the cartoon, and add points of your own.
5. Write notes for your overall evaluation of Source A. Make these bullet points rather than whole sentences.

Context for Source A

- Sir Charles Warren was Commissioner of Police, 1886–1888 (see pages 58–59 and 65–6).
- The police took firm action against riots in Trafalgar Square on Bloody Sunday (see pages 58–59).
- There were criticisms of police action on Bloody Sunday and accusations of police militarism (see pages 58–59).
- By 15 September there were four 'undiscovered' (unsolved) murders in Whitechapel (see pages 62–63).
- The killer used a knife (see pages 62–63).
- Warren had ordered huge increases in police patrols to try to catch the killer (see page 65).
- The CID investigations were thorough, but unsuccessful (see page 65).

Source A: A cartoon published in *Funny Folks*, 15 September, 1888. *Funny Folks* was a cheap weekly publication.

MILITARY DRILL v. POLICE DUTY.

Overall, the representation portrays the police as allowing the murderer to remain undiscovered, because Warren has the wrong priorities. Not enough is being done to concentrate on solving the murders.

Evaluating representations created by historians

Historians aim to give you their view of past events. The details in their writings are likely to be accurate. But you will still need to think about whether the view they give is the best one, depending on what you want to find out. If you want a detailed view of a period in depth, then a historian looking at overviews is not the best one for you.

Look back at the activity on page 66. You saw that what shapes a historian's work is what the historian wants to explore and what he or she is choosing to focus on.

The lions link to Trafalgar Square, where there are statues of lions. They are included as a reminder of police action on Bloody Sunday.

The gruesome figure of death can list his murders, unseen by the police, who are concentrating on other things.

Warren is being ridiculed – he is drawn on a hobby-horse.

The label 'militarism' suggests Warren wants to use the police like an army to control the people and restrict their liberties.

How effective was crime detection in late Victorian England?

Study Sources B and C on pages 69–70, thinking about the historian's focus. Even if two historians are both looking in depth or overview, they can still be looking for different things and so they have a different view. You can see that in Sources B and C. When you analyse and evaluate historians' representations, think about:

- the historian's focus
- the historian's view.

Activity

6. Study Sources B and C on pages 69–70. Copy this chart and complete it using as many of statements A–J as you choose. Write a statement in both columns if you think it belongs in both.

Symons (Source B)	Emsley (Source C)
Notes for my overall evaluation of the representations	

- **A.** The author is a historian who can write with authority.
- **B.** The author's focus is on how far the work of detectives changed.
- **C.** The author's focus is on fingerprinting as a scientific breakthrough which could change detective policing.
- **D.** The author's view is that advances were made which were important to progress in detection.
- **E.** The author's view is that little actually changed during the nineteenth century.
- **F.** This is a good representation of everyday approaches to policing.
- **G.** This is a good representation of how change in detective work came about.
- **H.** This representation, although accurate, is not complete because…
- **I.** The author provides detailed information to show how improvements came about.
- **J.** This representation does not include…

Source B: From *Crime and Detection: An Illustrated History*, Julian Symons, 1966. Symons was a historian and also a writer of crime fiction.

The greatest single scientific discovery made in forensic (detective) science was the realisation that every fingerprint shows markings that are unique. The credit for developing fingerprints into a system for criminal investigation in England belongs to Sir Edward Henry.

Sir Edward Henry devised the cataloguing system which became established throughout the world. He identified five basic patterns, gave them code numbers, and then broke down these main patterns into a great many subdivisions. In 1900 Henry's report to a London committee impressed them so much that fingerprinting was made the official criminal identification system in Britain. Sir Edward Henry was appointed head of the CID, and in 1903 became Police Commissioner.

Source C: The *Great British Bobby: A History of Policing from the Eighteenth Century to the Present*, Clive Emsley, 2009. Emsley is professor of history at the Open University.

…there had been no great developments in detection since the days of the Principal Officers of Bow Street [in the early nineteenth century]. Photographs had been available since the mid-nineteenth century; a system for cataloguing fingerprints was introduced in the 1890s and a Fingerprint Bureau was established at Scotland Yard in 1901. But both photographs and fingerprints required sophisticated cataloguing systems that enabled them to be easily and rapidly searched; these were not things that could be established overnight. Moreover it is clear that, well into the twentieth century, the daily *Police Gazette* that included photographs and descriptions of suspects … often remained unopened when it arrived at a … police station.

ResultsPlus
Top Tip

Remember, two students can come to different judgements about which representation is better and still get the same marks. The important thing is to be able to show that you have used criteria and can back up your decisions using the representations themselves and your own knowledge.

Symons and Emsley are both writing accurately and objectively, but they give us different views of changes in nineteenth century detective policing. How can they have different views and yet both be accurate? They can because their focus is different. One historian wants to show how much the work of the ordinary detective had actually changed in the nineteenth century; the other wants to show how new knowledge in science and technology made future advances in detection possible.

Add another criterion to use when evaluating representations: the purpose or focus of the author.

Activities

7. Create your own context box for these representations (Sources B and C). Add detail on:
   - the use of photography in nineteenth-century detective work
   - the use of the Bertillon system for identification and classification of criminals
   - the use of criminal records.

   You can add more points to your chart if you wish.

8. Which is the better representation of the effectiveness of Victorian policing? Produce a short oral statement or a PowerPoint presentation (to last about half a minute) to evaluate both representations, and give your judgement about which you think is better. Make your criteria clear. It will help if you use the vocabulary suggested on page 69.

Controlled assessment practice

9. Complete questions B (i) and (ii) below. Then turn to Maximise your marks, pages 74–78, to see if you need to improve your answer.

   B (i) Study Sources B and C on pages 69 and 70. They are both representations of Victorian policing.

   How far do these representations differ?

   B (ii) Study Sources B and C again and also Source A on page 68.

10. Choose the one you think is the best representation of how effective policing was in late-Victorian Britain. Explain your choice. You should use all three representations and your own knowledge to explain your answer.

Summary

- A historian's writing will usually be accurate and objective.
- Criteria must always be used when evaluating representations.
- The criteria could be: the accuracy, comprehensiveness, objectivity and purpose or focus of the representation.
- Representations must be evaluated in their historical context.

ResultsPlus
Maximise your marks

Part A Carry out a historical enquiry

In this task, you are required to carry out an enquiry; the enquiry focus will be set by Edexcel. The task is worth 20 marks and you should aim to spend about an hour writing it up. The mark scheme below shows how your work for this task will be marked.

Remember that in this task you are also assessed on the quality of your written communication: use historical terminology where appropriate, organise the information clearly and coherently, and make sure your spelling, punctuation and grammar are accurate.

Level	Answers at this level…	Marks available
Level 1	Make simple comments. There are few links between the comments and few details are given. Only one or two sources have been used in the enquiry.	1–5 marks
Level 2	Make statements about the enquiry topic. Information is included that is mostly relevant and accurate, but it is not well organised to focus on the point of the enquiry. A range of sources has been consulted and information taken from them.	6–10 marks
Level 3	Are organised to focus mainly on the point of the enquiry. Accurate and relevant information is given to support the points the student makes. A range of sources has been found and well-chosen material taken from them.	11–15 marks
Level 4	Focus well on the point of the enquiry. A well-supported conclusion is reached, for example about: the nature of change OR whether one factor was more important than the others OR the inter-relationship between two or more of the factors (depending on the enquiry focus). A range of sources appropriate to the enquiry has been identified and material from the sources has been well deployed.	16–20 marks

Let's look at an extract from one student's response to the following enquiry:

- The importance of the case of Derek Bentley

Student response

Doubts had been growing about the use of capital punishment for some time. In the 1950s there were more arguments about the death penalty. This was because people were worried about the case of Derek Bentley. He was sentenced to death for the murder of a policeman. He had committed a robbery with his friend Craig. Craig fired the gun, but he was too young to hang. Derek Bentley was 18. He was hanged in January 1953 although there were thousands of protestors outside the prison and 200 MPs signed a petition.

People were worried about hanging him because he had learning difficulties and he had not fired the shot. They were also worried about the case of Timothy Evans. He was executed, but Christie was the murderer they found out later. People also worried about the execution of Ruth Ellis because usually they did not hang women.

Ludovic Kennedy wrote a play called Murder Story. Derek's sister, Iris, said it was about Derek's case and the evil of capital punishment which he called legal killing.

Allan Todd says cases like Derek Bentley's made people focus on the death penalty. Many questioned the fairness of the system and people began to change their views about the death penalty. Only 13% of people were in favour of suspending the death penalty in 1948. 34% were in favour of suspending the death penalty in 1956. This evidence comes from mass observation public opinion surveys.

Silverman was an MP who founded the Campaign for the Abolition of the Death Penalty. He managed to persuade MPs in the House of Commons in 1948 to suspend the death sentence, but the House of Lords did not allow it. In 1953 he wrote a book called Hanged and Innocent about the case of Derek Bentley (Spartacus website).

The case of Derek Bentley was important. It led to widespread national debate in newspapers, on television and radio about the use of the death penalty. Derek Bentley was given an official government pardon in 1998 which did not help him much 46 years too late. The New Abolitionist Newsletter said that his case was pivotal in bringing about the end of capital punishment in Britain. In 1965 capital punishment was suspended for five years except for treason, piracy with violence and arson in Royal Dockyards which most people do not do! In 1969 parliament confirmed the abolition of capital punishment for murder.

Moderator comment

This extract indicates that the response would gain a mark in level 2. The student describes changes in ideas about the death penalty. The student also describes worries about controversial cases and reactions to the Derek Bentley case. Comments are made about the importance of the Bentley case – 'made people focus on the death penalty'; 'pivotal in bringing about an end to capital punishment' – but these have been taken from the student's notes and have not been further developed.

The student has used a good range of sources. Text books, internet sites and other sources have been used to provide information. Material has been selected for relevance and the student has combined notes from different sources. However, the material has not been smoothly integrated and phrases have often been copied directly from text into notes and from notes into the response. This means that the student cannot be given high marks in level 2 for quality of written communication.

To improve the response, the student should focus more centrally on the precise enquiry: the importance of the case of Derek Bentley. The student could show importance by looking at:

- increased worry over the use of the death penalty
- the work of individuals who campaigned as a result of the case
- the influence of campaign groups
- the importance of other factors which show that the Bentley case was not alone in bringing about the end of the death penalty.

Additionally, the material should be better organised in the student's own words rather than simply joined together from notes.

ResultsPlus
Maximise your marks

Let's look at an extract from an improved student response.

Improved student response

The importance of the Derek Bentley case came mainly from the 'unease' (Christoph) it caused in much of the general public and the fact that it encouraged people to campaign against the death penalty. Well-known journalists like Ludovic Kennedy and MPs like Sidney Silverman campaigned. They also published books and plays. The play 'Murder Story' was based on Derek's case according to his sister in her book 'Let Him Have Justice'. This would make people think, especially since she says Ludovic Kennedy called capital punishment 'legal killing'. Silverman's book 'Hanged and Innocent' also made people think – which explains why Allan Todd says that cases like Derek Bentley's made people focus on the death penalty. It made people ask whether it was right to use a death penalty when it could mean that someone who had not actually fired the gun, and didn't really have the mental age to be properly aware of what was going on, could be 'legally killed'.

As a result many began to change their views about the death penalty. We know from Mass Observation Surveys of public opinion that between 1948 and 1956 the percentage of people in favour of suspending the death penalty increased from 13% to 34%. This is like a growing circle – people were uneasy, books were written and the campaigns developed, so more people began to focus on the death penalty, so the campaigns grew and so more people took notice of them. Of course, it was not just the Bentley case, though the New Abolitionist calls it 'pivotal', meaning it was the one most important in changing minds. But the Timothy Evans case made people worry about miscarriages of justice because there an innocent man was hanged. And the Mass Observation Survey suggests that the Ellis Case had most influence in 1956 – though that might just have been because it was very fresh in people's minds...

Overall the case of Derek Bentley was important because it made many people begin to question the death penalty. It stirred up a campaign which had been 'dormant'. It was a case which helped to change attitudes in the public. It was probably the most important because it kicked the campaign into action.

Part B(i) Compare two representations

In this task, you are required to analyse and compare two representations of history. The task is worth 10 marks and you should aim to spend about 30 minutes writing it up. The mark scheme below shows how your work for this task will be marked.

Level	Answers at this level...	Marks available
Level 1	Identify the main features of the two representations by giving descriptions, direct quotations or paraphrases from one or both representations.	1–3 marks
Level 2	Identify the differences in two representations by comparing similarities and/or differences in their details.	4–7 marks
Level 3	Show understanding of the similarities and/or differences in the way the past is represented in the two extracts. The answer uses precisely selected detail from the two representations to support the explanations and the judgement about how far the representations differ.	8–10 marks

Let's look at an extract from one student's response.

Study sources B and C on pages 69–70. They are both representations of how effective policing was in late Victorian Britain. How far do these representations differ? (10 marks)

Student response

Representations B and C are both about fingerprints. Julian Symons says it was the greatest single discovery made in detective science. Sir Edward Henry developed it into a system for criminal investigation by giving the patterns code numbers so it could be the official criminal identification system. Representation B gives us more information about Sir Edward Henry who developed the system. In Representation C Clive Emsley agrees that a system for cataloging fingerprints was begun in the 1890s, but he doesn't say who did it. He also includes photographs which Symons does not include in Representation B. But Emsley says there were no great developments in detection because these were not things which could be established overnight. So overall they differ quite a bit, because Representation B talks about great discoveries and Representation C says there were no great developments.

ResultsPlus
Maximise your marks

Moderator comment

In this part of the answer, the student has comprehended the details in the representations and is comparing them. We can see the language of comparison is used: 'Both about', 'more information', 'agrees', 'does not include', 'differ quite a bit'.

The student has noted the details which are similar in both sources and also where one author provides details which the other has not included. The student has also noted that there is a disagreement about how much development in detection there had been.

There is enough comprehension and comparison for the answer to get into level 2, but the answer concentrates mainly on differences in details in the two sources. To raise the response to the next level, the answer should show more awareness of the differences in the portrayal of developments in detection in these two representations. Representation B's focus is on discoveries in detective science and Symons portrays fingerprinting as a great advance. Representation C's focus is on what detectives actually did and he concludes that there were no great developments, because the new technology by itself could not change detectives' work in practice. The student notes that 'these were not things which could be established overnight', but has only taken these words from the source. This aspect of the response should be much more developed.

Let's look at an improved version of this answer.

Improved student response

Representations B and C are both about fingerprints. Julian Symons says it was the greatest single discovery made in detective science. Sir Edward Henry developed it into a system for criminal investigation by giving the patterns code numbers so it could be the official criminal identification system. Representation B gives us more information about Sir Edward Henry who developed the system. In Representation C Clive Emsley agrees that a system for cataloging fingerprints was begun in the 1890s, but he doesn't say who did it. He also mentions photographs became available which Symons does not mention in Representation B. But Emsley says there were no great developments in actual detection though he does tells us that the fingerprint bureau was set up in 1901 which suggests that some use of fingerprints was being made by detectives at Scotland Yard. The big difference between Representation B and C is what they are focusing on. Symons is looking at a scientific breakthrough which made a new system of criminal identification possible – this means he is able to talk about a great discovery. Emsley on the other hand is looking at what detectives actually did in practice. He implies that detectives didn't even bother to open the Police Gazette, although they could see photographs and descriptions of suspects. This suggests that photographs did not have a big impact on detective work in the nineteenth century either. Emsley includes an important point – that without a sophisticated cataloguing system, photographic or fingerprint evidence could not be easily searched. Which meant it could not be easily used by detectives because these cataloguing systems were not things which could be established overnight. The representations agree that a new means of identifying criminals using fingerprints was developed at the end of the nineteenth century, but their portrayal of policing differs quite a bit, because Representation B gives the impression of great improvements with the focus on great discoveries but Representation C gives the impression of no great developments.

Part B(ii) Analyse and evaluate three representations

In this task, you are required to analyse and evaluate three representations of history. The task is worth 20 marks and you should aim to spend about an hour writing it up. The mark scheme below shows how your work for this task will be marked. Remember that in this task you are also assessed on the quality of your written communication: use historical terminology where appropriate, organise the information clearly and coherently, and make sure your spelling, punctuation and grammar are accurate.

Level	Answers at this level...	Marks available
Level 1	Show some understanding of the main features of the sources and select material. Simple judgements are made about the representation, and a limited amount of accurate information about the period is given. The material is not detailed; links between the information and the representation are not explicit.	1–5 marks
Level 2	Show an understanding of the main features of the three sources and select key features of the representations from them. Judgement is made about the best representation and detailed and accurate information about the period is added. There is little linkage between description and judgement. Judgements may relate to the accuracy or comprehensiveness of the representation.	6–10 marks
Level 3	Analyse the three sources and show some of the ways in which the past situation has been represented. Detail from the sources is used to support the analysis. There is a critical evaluation of each representation based on well selected information about the period and at least two clear criteria are applied, for example, the author's purpose or objectivity, or the accuracy, comprehensiveness of the representation.	11–15 marks
Level 4	Analyse the three sources to show the way in which the past situation has been represented. Precisely selected detail from the sources is used to support the analysis. There is a critical evaluation of the representation based on precisely selected information about the period and applying at least three criteria, for example the author's purposes or objectivity, or the comprehensiveness and/or accuracy of the representation.	16–20 marks

Let's look at an extract from one student's response.

Study Sources A, B and C on pages 68–70.

Choose the one which you think is the best Representation of how effective policing was in late Victorian Britain. Explain your choice. You should use all three representations and your own knowledge to explain your answer. (20 marks)

Student response

I think Representation A is useful because it shows what people thought about the police at the time of the Ripper murders. But it's not complete because it's only about the Jack the Ripper case. And it's not very accurate because we know that Sir Charles Warren ordered huge increases in police patrols to try and catch the killer.

I think Representation B is useful because it tells us about the development of fingerprinting. It tells us that Sir Edward Henry developed a system which became used throughout the world. But it doesn't tell us much about what detectives actually did, so it is not comprehensive.

I think Representation C is the best. It gives us accurate information about the development of fingerprinting. It doesn't mention Sir Edward Henry, but it tells us the fingerprint bureau was set up in Scotland Yard. This is the best representation of how effective policing was because it tells us what the police actually did. It tells us that not much changed at all really in detection. There was new technology, but the ordinary detective couldn't really use it.

Moderator comment

The student has made a short comment which identifies the information which each representation can provide. The comment that Representation A 'shows what people thought about the police' should be further developed to consider what we can learn about police effectiveness from this. The student has begun to use some criteria to evaluate the representations, but none of the comments are developed very far. The student uses the criterion of accuracy to evaluate Representation A. This is a good choice of a criterion by which to evaluate a cartoon. But the student uses only a limited amount of own knowledge to test accuracy and does not make clear which parts of Representation A make it 'not very accurate'. To improve the answer, the student should make more use of contextual knowledge and analyse the cartoon more fully to show its inaccuracy.

In evaluating Representations B and C, the student has chosen a valid criterion for the best representation of the effectiveness of policing – what the sources tell us about 'what detectives actually did'. Here the student is basing the judgement on the focus of the representations, though this should be made more explicit. However the student's comments need to make much more use of contextual knowledge – particularly in relation to 'what detectives actually did' since the student uses this criterion to evaluate Representation B as 'not comprehensive' and Representation C as 'best'.

To reach the highest level the student must also make use of more criteria – three should be used to rate each representation.

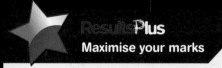

Maximise your marks

Let's look at extracts from an improved student response.

Improved student response

Representation A portrays the police as ineffective. It shows the Ripper murderer with a list of murders which he has been able to get away with. The cartoonist has chosen to make Sir Charles Warren, the police commissioner, look ridiculous, riding a hobby horse. He has placed the commissioner and the police in Trafalgar square, shown by the lions. He has used the label 'militarism' to suggest that Sir Charles Warren is more interested in running his force as a little army to keep demonstrators in order. While he concentrates on that sort of thing, the murderer isn't caught. This portrays the police as ineffective because they are not concentrating on the right things. The cartoon is designed to be critical, not objective – and it has left out important information. It has not taken account of the huge number of police which Sir Charles put on patrol, which Belton Cobb tells us he did. Representation A is partially accurate. The murderer wasn't caught. And we know there were criticisms of the way Sir Charles ran the police force. He was accused of worrying too much about uniforms and drilling and discipline even before the murders. But he was given the job because he was a soldier, and because people thought that the police needed more discipline. So although it may be accurate that he increased the amount of drilling and there was more militarism, it is not fair to imply by this that the police are concentrating on the wrong things and letting a murderer escape. Furthermore the cartoon was published at a time of moral panic over the Ripper murders, so it is not really a typical portrayal of Victorian policing. Other sources such as the 'famous figures of London' card suggest that there was trust in the police and the job they did …

Representation C is better than Representation B when dealing with the effectiveness of the detective force. Representation B portrays fingerprinting as a breakthrough, but we know that the first case in England where a criminal was convicted using fingerprint evidence was not until 1902. So this is not the best representation of how effective policing was before 1901, though it is accurate that fingerprinting was an advance in the methods of detection. Representation C's focus is on what actually changed in detection, but it has limitations. The view it gives us of 'little change in detection' is only dealing with new technology. It is looking at how far the new technology was actually used by the police and whether it could actually be used. In other ways detection did change and improve. We know that detective divisions were increased and arrest rates improved in the nineteenth century …

Although Representation C is not a comprehensive picture of the effectiveness of policing, overall it seems to be the best. Its focus is on what actually changed in detection, which makes it better than Representation B. It gives an overview and aims to be objective. This makes it much better than Representation A, which is not strictly accurate, is exaggerated and is limited to London in one untypical year.

Glossary

Beat: the set route a police constable patrolled. He was expected to average about 2.5 miles per hour.

Capital punishment: the death penalty – executing (killing) a person as a punishment for a crime.

CID: Criminal Investigations Department of the police.

Crime Prevention Panels: locally organised groups who work with the police to deal with local crime problems.

Fascists: members of an extreme far-right political group that opposes democracy and believes the state should have total power. It is often associated with racism.

Flogging: a harsh form of corporal punishment that was used for serious rule breaking.

Flying pickets: strikers travelling to protest in other areas where miners were still working.

Forensic science: using scientific methods and knowledge to discover facts that can be used in detecting crime.

Fraud: using deception (trickery) to get a personal advantage or to harm another person.

Habitual criminals: people who often commit crimes.

Home Secretary: a senior member of the government, in charge of the Home Office.

Humane: using kindness, mercy and compassion.

Identifiers: ways of proving a criminal's identity by recording their photographs and five key measurements such as head length and middle-finger length.

Loyalists: Irish people who strongly support political union between Great Britain and Northern Ireland.

Marksman: a person who is skilled in accurate shooting of a firearm.

Moral panic: a short time when the public is full of panic, thinking that a group or individual is a threat to society.

Neighbourhood Watch: an organised group of citizens who work together with the police to prevent crime within their neighbourhood.

Posthumous pardon: being found not guilty after having been executed.

Rehabilitate: to restore to useful life.

Republicans: Irish people who believe strongly that Ireland should be reunited as a single country, independent of Great Britain.

Trade union: an organisation in which workers group together, usually to negotiate pay and conditions with employers.

Victim Support Schemes: local branches of a national organisation which exists to help people who have been victims of crime.

Published by Pearson Education Limited, a company incorporated in England and Wales, having its registered office at Edinburgh Gate, Harlow, Essex, CM20 2JE. Registered company number: 872828

Edexcel is a registered trademark of Edexcel Limited

Text © Pearson Education Limited

First published 2010

12 11 10

10 9 8 7 6 5 4 3 2 1

British Library Cataloguing in Publication Data

A catalogue record for this book is available from the British Library

ISBN 978 1 846906 46 6

Typeset by Pantek Arts Ltd

Original illustrations © Pearson Education Ltd 2010

Printed in Great Britain at Scotprint, Haddington

Acknowledgements

We would like to thank Helen Johnston, Chris Williams and Maggie Smith for their invaluable help in the development of this material.

Martyn Whittock would like to thank the following people for all of their interest and support: Mary and John, Joy and Eddie, Mary and Haydn, Sheila and Geoffrey, Joan and Sandy.

Picture credits

The publisher would like to thank the following for their kind permission to reproduce their photographs:

(Key: b-bottom; c-centre; l-left; r-right; t-top)

akg-images Ltd: British Library 38; **Alamy Images:** Homer Sykes Archive 15, Rodger Tamblyn 2; **Bridgeman Art Library Ltd:** Robert Sauber 54; **National Gallery of Canada:** Alphonse Bertillon 57; **Corbis:** Hulton-Deutsch Collection 17, Stacy Morrison 34, STEPHEN HIRD / Reuters 18; **© Crown Copyright / Office of Public Sector Information:** HM Prison Service 9; **FotoLibra:** Brendan Montgomery's collection 28; **Getty Images:** Manchester Daily Express / Contributor 23tr, Hulton Archive / Stringer 6br, 7, Steve Eason / Stringer 24; **Angela Leonard:** 61; **Metropolitan Police Authority:** Metropolitan Police Authority 2009 37tr/2, 37br; **National Library of Australia:** 6tr; **Newspaper Library, the British Library:** 58, 68; **Images of the Past:** 6cr; **John Wright Photography:** 8; **Photolibrary. com:** Jewish Chronical / Imagestate RM 23br, Rod Edwards / Britain on View 60; **Photoshot Holdings Limited:** UPPA 31; **Punch Cartoon Library:** 56, 62; **Report Digital:** John Harris 51; **Rex Features:** Richard Gardner 13, Geoffrey Swaine 19; **TopFoto:** Topham / PA 33, The British Library / HIP / TopFoto 63; **Barts and The London NHS Trust:** 42

Cover images: *Front:* **TopFoto:** Sennecke / Ullsteinbild

All other images © Pearson Education

Every effort has been made to trace the copyright holders and we apologise in advance for any unintentional omissions. We would be pleased to insert the appropriate acknowledgement in any subsequent edition of this publication.

Text

We are grateful to the following for permission to reproduce copyright material:

Extract on page 51 from *People in Change*, 0-582-22665-1, Longman (Josh Brooman 1994) page 80; Extract on page 30 from *Combating terrorism: the Northern Ireland experience (The Royal Constabulary and the Terrorist Threat*, 978-0-4153-6733-2, Routledge (James Dingley) pages 181-182; Extract on page 47 from The Fight for Derek Bentley, A Full Pardon - 46 Years Later, by Marlene Martin, The New Abolitionist Newsletter, November 1998, Vol. II, Issue 5, http://www.nodeathpenalty.org/newab009/bentley.html; Extract on page 55 from *English Police*, 978-0-5822-5768-9, Longman (Clive Emsley 1996) page 259; Extract on page 14 from Community Sentencing, http://www.direct.gov.uk/en/CrimeJusticeAndTheLaw/PrisonAndProbation/DG_070333, © Crown Copyright; Extract on page 30 from *The Edge of the Union: The Ulster Loyalist Political Vision*, 978-0-1982-7976-1, Oxford University Press (Steve Bruce 1994) page 125; Extract on page 43 from Doctor Crippen may have been innocent, October 17, 2007, http://www.timesonline.co.uk/tol/news/uk/crime/article2674601.ece, © NI Syndication; Extract on page 46 from *CA11 British Society StudentBook* 9781846906442, Pearson Education (Nigel Bushnell and Cathy Warren 2010) pages 26-27; Extract on page 48 from *Let him have Justice*, 0-330-34399-8, Macmillan (Iris Bentley 1996) page 185, Iris Bentley, 1996; Extract on page 48 from *Allan Todd Crime Punishment and Protest*, 0521-00661-9, Cambridge University Press (2002) pages 172-173, Allan Todd, Crime Punishment and Protest, 2002, Cambridge University Press; Quote on page 52 from Margaret Thatcher 30/05/1984, Copyright Margaret Thatcher. Reproduced with permission from www.margaretthatcher.org, the official website of the Margaret Thatcher Foundation; Extract on page 52 from *The End of an Era: Diaries 1980-1990*, 0-09-997110-0, Arrow Books Ltd (Tony Benn 1994) page 356; Extract on page 56 from *Crime and Criminals of Victorian London*, 1-8607-7392-3, Phillimore & Co (Adrian Gray 2006) page 8; Extract on page 57 from *English Police* 0-5822-5768-9, Longman (Clive Emsley 1996) page 73; Extract on page 64 from *Jack the Ripper The Definitive History*, 1-4058-0712-1, Pearson Longman (Paul Begg 2005) page 70; Extract on page 65 from *Jack The Ripper The Definitive History*, 978-1-4058-0712-8, Pearson Longman (Paul Begg 2005) page 72; Extract on page 65 from *Jack the Ripper The Definitive History* 978-1-4058-0712-8 (Paul Begg 2005) page 75; Extract on page 70 and 74 from *The Great British Bobby A History of Policing from the Eighteenth Century to the Present*, 978-1-8472-4947-0, Quercus (Clve Emsley 2009) pages 166-167; Extract on page 48 from British Journalist, Ludovic Kennedy, Dies at 89, New York Times Europe Robert D. McFadden, October 21, 2009, © PARS International Corp; Extract on page 13 from *Punishment in the Community, Managing Offenders, Making Choices*, (Anne Worrall and Clare Hoy 2005), Willan Publishing, 978-1-8439-2076-2, page 140; Extract on page 55 from *Crime and Justice 1750-1950*, (Barry Godfrey and Paul Lawrence 2005), Willan Publishing, 978-1-8439-2116-5, page 19; Extract on page 64 from *Crime and Justice 1750-1950*, (Barry Godfrey and Paul Lawrence 2005), Willan Publishing, 978-1-8439-2116-5, page 93; Extract on page 65 from *Critical Years at the Yard* (Belton Cobb 1956), Faber and Faber, B0007IXCIM, page 226; Extract on page 69 and 74 from *Crime and Detection An Illustrated History* (Julian Symons 1966) Panther Books Ltd, B0000CN7C2, HarperCollins, page 78-80 ; Extract on page 47 *Capital Punishment and British Politics* (James B. Christoph 1962) George Allen & Unwin, B0016CS7QA, HarperCollins, pages 99, 105, 107

In some instances we have been unable to trace the owners of copyright material, and we would appreciate any information that would enable us to do so.

Websites

The websites used in this book were correct and up to date at the time of publication. It is essential for tutors to preview each website before using it in class so as to ensure that the URL is still accurate, relevant and appropriate. We suggest that tutors bookmark useful websites and consider enabling students to access them through the school/college intranet.

Disclaimer

This material has been published on behalf of Edexcel and offers high-quality support for the delivery of Edexcel qualifications. This does not mean that the material is essential to achieve any Edexcel qualification, nor does it mean that it is the only suitable material available to support any Edexcel qualification. Edexcel material will not be used verbatim in setting any Edexcel examination or assessment. Any resource lists produced by Edexcel shall include this and other appropriate resources.

Copies of official specifications for all Edexcel qualifications may be found on the Edexcel website: www.edexcel.com